Four Steps to Manhood.
Interest, Discovery, Lust and Love.

By C N Wilde

Introduction

Maid, wife, or harlot, she will bid you wait:

The females instinct is to hesitate...

Don Juan's Note Book

It never ceases to amaze me, as men, how stupid we really are. We spend our whole lives searching for one thing while all the time really wanting another. Someone once said that if men didn't spend their whole lives chasing sex they would live longer. What a stupid thing to research and want an even more stupid thing to publish! You can bet it was a woman, or more likely a group of women, who carried out that useful piece of research. No matter how true this may or may not be I know it will not change one single mans life. Sex is the one thing that drives us on, makes us get up in the morning, go to work simply so we can get money to go chasing sex. But although we may need this on a minute by minute basis it is love that we really crave. Not simply the someone to wake up next to each morning kind of love, not the someone to make us breakfast and wash our shirts kind of love, of course this is nice but far too simple. We want that Romeo and Juliet kind of love that we learn about in school, that romantic dinners and nights by an open log fire kind of love. But is it possible to merge these two things and live happily ever after? No of course it isn't, it's impossible. That is the dilemma we as men have to live with on a day to day basis. This book charts the voyage of one such man as he struggles to come to terms with something his father forgot to tell him about.

Susan

We were sisters then in that long summer
of sunshine and sensation

Liliane James

It starts a little earlier than puberty when you first begin to notice the difference between boys and girls. School is a wonderful time of life no worries in the world, no bills to pay and no mouths to feed. Of course it also provides you with your first opportunity to explore these inexplicable differences between you and the opposite sex.

It was third grade and Susan was the most beautiful blond hared eight year old you have ever seen. She lived next-door to the school and her house had a gate right into the playground. I always thought that would be so cool because it would mean not having to get up so early every morning. How I hated getting up early in the morning. The downside of this was that her mother was a teacher at the school. Of course on balance getting up early didn't seem so bad compared to having your mother know everything that went on. Her mother was a grey haired slender women who always looked immaculate in her suits and I used to fantasise that she was exactly the type of women I would like to marry. Of course I didn't know at the time about the old saying 'look at the mother to find out what the daughter will be like,' but on reflection it would seem my instincts were correct. That summer proved though that having a gate from the playground to your house could have other advantages.

We all used to enjoy watching the girls skip rope at lunch time and wondering how it was they managed to get their underwear so tight and still remain comfortable but I concluded that if I continued to watch maybe I would figure it out. Besides there was something rather fascinating discovering what colour their panties were that day but I couldn't quite put my finger on why it was so intriguing.

Unlike most of the boys I didn't just have male friends, in fact more than half were girls and for reasons I can't really remember I just seemed to slip into spending most of my time with them, much to the envy of my classmates. Whenever one of the boys in the class thought he liked a girl someone made sure I knew and in this way they could be assured that particular girl found out. I guess it was a bit of a power trip really.

Susan became the first real love of my life. Wherever one went the other was always there making sure they weren't missing out on anything. By the end of that first summer we'd even begun to develop an unspoken understanding of what the other was thinking. It is strange to think back and realise just how wonderful an experience that was to have so early in life. To be able to look across a room and know exactly what the other was thinking without even speaking. We also talked all the time about everything and anything. Where we would like to live when we grew up, what sort of house we should live in and how many children we were going to have. (We decided two was more than enough, besides it was much more difficult to get a good table in a restaurant for five). What I didn't know at the time was this was to be an emerging pattern that would go on repeating itself throughout my life.

As you can imagine we were the talk of the school, laughingly known as the old married couple, we used to lap it up. I'm surprised her mother seemed to know nothing about it, maybe she didn't know everything that went on after all. We began spending afternoons together and this is where my sexual education really began. Susan loved to play games and dressing up was one of her favourites. She adored role playing and would delight in putting on her fairy princess outfit, I of course was Peter Pan, and then climbing up one of the old breech trees that separated their yard from the school and pretending she was on her way to Never Never Land.

Then there was the Indian Princess outfit, yes you guessed it I was the cowboy. It always started off with me chasing her round the yard yelling it was time to surrender before we burnt down the village and killed all the women and children. However it somehow always ended with me tired to a tree. Now to this day I cannot for the life of me remember how this started or how it was that this little slip of a girl managed to get me tired to a tree each time but tired I was and completely helpless. This situation seemed to delight Susan and she used to make me do certain things before she would let me go like sing some stupid song which she knew I hated or confess my undying love for her.

It was during one of these games that she decided that my saying I loved her was just not enough and without any ceremony pulled my shorts down to reveal my boyhood in all it glory. Well I was devastated, never before had I been so humiliated. I struggled valiantly to get loose but she was just too good at tying knots and the more I struggled the more she laughed. Eventually the laughter subsided and she decided she had better untie me before her mother came home and found me naked, tied to a tree in the back garden. As soon as I was loose I pulled up my shorts, screamed some obscenities at her, which were pretty weak since I didn't know very many, and raced home. To this day my mother still doesn't know why I came in so hot and troubled that afternoon, refusing point blank to eat my supper, instead escaping to my room to nurse my humiliation. As I lay in bed that night I plotted my revenge she wasn't doing to get away with this.

The next day everything went as normal. In fact, unbelievably, she acted as if nothing had happened the afternoon before, how was that possible? She had pulled my shorts down and totally humiliated me for Christ's sake! It was a wonder the whole school didn't know by now yet despite my paranoia nobody said anything. Well at least it seemed I could trust her to keep her mouth shut. As per usual I ended up at Susan's place after school. But this afternoon was going to be my afternoon. When she went to change I waited a minute or so and then ever so quietly slipped up the stairs until I was just outside her bedroom. I peered round the door and waited until she began to pull her uniform off over her head then sprang into the room and pinned her to the bed. She was helpless and she was mine. Despite her struggle I managed to find the elastic of her panties and pulled them off in one movement.

"There see how you like that," I yelled, "that will teach you to go pulling my shorts down while I'm helpless to do anything about it."

But what I saw was not what I expected. Instead of a dangly thing with a bit of skin under it her bum seemed to continue all the way around, fascinating. And so it was I saw my first girls bits.

Susan on the other hand was not put off by this at all. As soon as I let her go she simply finished taking off her uniform and stood there looking at me with a smile on her face. What, I thought, no crying and yelling? No, not Susan in fact she took great delight in striding round the room with nothing on but and pair of white socks.

"Well what do you think then?" she ventured. "Am I more pretty than the other girls?"

"I don't know," the words sort of falling out of my mouth.

"What do you mean you don't know?"

"Well I haven't seen any other girls without clothes on before have I?"

"That's not what Clare told me she said you striped in her bedroom last week after her birthday party."

"Well that's a complete lie I never did anything of the sort."

"You had better be telling me the truth Charles Wilde or I'm going to tell everyone I pulled your shorts down while you were tied to a tree in my backyard."

"Oh yer well I'll just tell them you paraded round your room with nothing but your socks on then."

"No one is ever going to believe that but I bet they will believe me." Her eyes widened a little, was starting to get mad.

I sat and thought about this for a moment, she was absolutely right, I would never be able to show my face again in the play ground. She stood there with her hands on her little waist almost willing me to argue the point but I was having none of it, she wasn't going to catch me out that easily. I figured that while we were in a situation which no one was ever going to believe happened I may as well make the most it and my curiosity began to take over. I asked her to do all sorts of poses which despite her protests she seemed to take great pleasure in performing. I think it was all part of the acting thing.

In fact she spent the entire afternoon wandering about the house wearing nothing, me in toe of course, before hearing the gate go signalling her mothers return. She hastily slipped on her fairy princess outfit, not bothering with any underwear, and skipped down stairs to greet her mother as if nothing had happened. I on the other hand experienced my first real feelings of intense guilt and on coming down stairs tripped on the bottom step and landed flat on my face in the hallway, to this day my nose has never been the same. Flustered and wanting very badly to get out of there I made my apologies and left as quickly as I could.

Each day we repeated that first afternoons antics, I would wait until she went up stairs to change, sneak up the stairs to surprise her, wait until she had her uniform off and run into the room and pin her to the bed. This went on for months even to the point of her always selecting the fairy princess outfit when she heard her mother coming home. Looking back I think it was because in this outfit she looked most like butter wouldn't melt in her mouth, all the better for ensuring her mother suspected nothing. I could even manage to make it down the stairs in one piece. I looked forward to these afternoons more and more. It was several repeat performances of this scenario though before she realised her new found power over me, much stronger than tying me to a tree, and she seemed intrigued to find out just how far she could push her luck.

One afternoon I found myself having milk and cookies at the kitchen table while her mother began to prepare dinner. Susan sat there grinning like a Cheshire Cat, I began to feel extremely uncomfortable. She started to mouth something under her breath. At first I couldn't tell what she was saying but with dawning horror I finally made out the words 'I'm going to tell'. I should have realised what I was getting into before this. My stomach began to turn over and I started to feel very sick. It was time to leave. The next day she apologised for being so cruel but there was a gleam in her eye I didn't much care for and I was in no mood for apologies. I hadn't slept a wink that night wondering if she was going to tell her mother what had been going on, as it turned out she never did.

Thus we see the beginning of the fall of mankind. Anyone who tells you little girls know nothing about sex and have no awareness of their sexuality doesn't know what they are talking about. As soon as girls discover they can use their sex as a method of getting what they want there is no stopping them. Unfortunately Susan was a basically a good girl and despite my pleading it never went any further. Unlike Heide. Heide was my kind of girl.

By the time I was ten I was dying to find out more about sex and it dominated all the discussion at school, but more especially amongst the girls. They were as fascinated or should I say more fascinated then we were about the subject and used to spend hours discussing what they had or hadn't seen while peering through the keyhole of the bathroom at their brothers. I remember one particularly interesting story relayed by Kate. Kate had an older brother, almost a man at 15, he always seemed to have friends over to stay which provided Kate with a great source of information. It would seem that one particular weekend their parents went away and left Jeff in charge for the first time. It was inevitable, therefore, that Saturday night there was going to be a party and so it was. Jeff invited ten of his friends around for what he told Kate was to be a quiet night in watching videos, what ensued was something very different.

Everyone began turning up around 7 pm. Kate had been given strict instructs to stay upstairs in her bedroom which she felt was extremely unfair but at least it provided a good vantage point for watching the comings and goings. As the night progressed and the music got louder she soon grew bored of being in her room and decided a look downstairs was in order. She positioned herself on the stairs where she had a good view of the sitting room and proceeded to take in all the details. Everyone was up dancing and singing and generally enjoying themselves as she suspected and there seemed to be plenty of drinking going on. Then just as she began to think about going back to bed someone put a slow song on and turned the lights down. She said everyone was paired up and one by one began to kiss as they danced. Kate found this a little bit more interesting, perhaps more interesting than she was willing to admit at the time as she was yet to find someone who she could try this out on and decided to stay put for a little while longer.

"Well I just wanted to try and see who my brother was kissing that's all," she said defensively.

"Yer right," rang the echo round the people listening.

Just before the song finished one of her brother mates appeared from the sitting room with a very pretty girl on his arm, whom she didn't recognise, and proceeded towards the stairs, it was time to beat a hasty retreat. She ran back to her bedroom leaving the door ajar so she could still watch. They came up the stairs and headed straight for her room. Rather than diving into bed however she decided to hide in the closet for some reason.

"What the hell were you thinking about hiding in the closet?," Anne asked in that little whinny voice she had.

"Look I don't know it just happened all right? And besides I'm sure glad I did otherwise I wouldn't be standing here telling you this story."

They came in, turning the light on as they went, and fell onto her bed kissing. She stood very still trying not to breathe, all the time watching through the slats in her wardrobe door. Within minutes they began to take each others clothes off. When they were completely naked the boy began to suck on the girls breasts. Kate could not explain why she said she thought only babies did that but the girl seemed to like it all the same. Then he slid down between the girls legs and started making all these slurping noises. Kate said the girl just lay there with a huge grin on her face, her eyes closed, every so often saying things like 'yes just there that's it.' She was actually quite a good story teller and as she recounted this bit she rolled her head back and mimicked the girls voice. Eventually he came up and rolled on his back and Kate saw what she described as the biggest dick she had ever seen. The girl then took it in her mouth and started sucking the end of it like a lollipop. This drew a cry of 'oh yuk' from the others listening.

"How could anyone even think of doing that?" piped up Anne again.

I was starting to grow impatient. "Look just everyone shut up and let her get on with the story OK?"

"After what seemed like an age she finally came up, kissed her way up his chest and promptly sat on his dick!"

Kate by this time was looking somewhat flushed and concluded her story by explaining that his dick must have stuck right up inside her because as she then began to bounce up and down on it you could see it disappearing inside her. There was great disbelief expressed at this point.

"How on earth could you stick something inside you like that and still be alive?"

Sometimes that girl just made me so mad. "Anne she saw it all right? Perhaps if you spent some time watching what goes on around you instead of reading all those books we could listen to a story of yours one day but until that happens let her finish will you?"

Actually she had finished. Apart from a general description of how the girl had played with his dick as it shrunk, after she finally got off him, they eventually left. She had managed to make it through the entire episode without being discovered.

As this story was retold and retold around the school that week it grew even more unbelievable, as you can imagine, until I overheard Kevin telling Mark that the boys dick was more that a foot long and when she dropped down on him her split became even longer until it almost reached her belly button. At this telling Mark's face turned ashen. Mind you Kevin was always one for a good story. One day we were sitting in class and a note appeared on my desk from Alex who sat next to me. When Miss Worphole turned round to the board to start the comprehension lesson I opened it up and read.

DO NOT PASS THIS TO ANY GIRLS!

it had written across the top in capital letters.

MISSY HAS FORGOTTEN TO PUT ON ANY UNDERWEAR TODAY.
KEVIN.

We spent the entire lunch break positioning ourselves around the play ground such that when Missy walked by we could easily lay down on our backs and look up her dress. I personally saw nothing but Kevin swore till the end of that term that he had seen the lot.

Susan came up to me in the playground some weeks later and announced she had something to tell me so we made our way to the back of the sports oval for some privacy.

"I'm leaving," she said, "Mum thinks it would be better for me if I started at the girls school next term, she says that hopefully it will take my mind of boys."

She began crying. I was devastated. How was I going to live without her? Didn't her mother realise what she was doing? I guess if the truth is known she probably did. On the last day mum came and picked me up at the school gate. I stood holding Susan while everyone watched until finally mum had to take my arm and drag me away. The tears in my eyes welled up and spilled over, running down my cheeks. During those next few weeks I felt truly alone for the first time. I have always wondered what happened to her and lost count of the times I hung around hoping to see her. I never did.

Heide

To move as one between desire and shame suspended.
Percy Bysshe Shelley

At thirteen Heide was two years older than me. Borne in Hungry, not only did she have a dark and mysterious air about her she was an older woman and therefore very desirable. She lived six doors down and would frequently come up to my place to help with the horses and in fact that's how we met. One afternoon I was coming back from Susan's house, wandering along in a day dream and practically knocked her over as she stood watching the horses. After much apologising I told her my name was Charles and we got talking about the horses. I thought it strange at first that we'd never met, surely my eyesight was not that bad yet. It transpired however that she'd just moved to the area and the first thing she'd done was come to see the horses. She said she loved riding and took lessons ever week in Suffolk where she used to live and did my father give lessons? I had to explain that they were his pride and joy and he and my mother were the only ones allowed to ride them.

"Pity," she said, "it would have been fun to go riding with you. Perhaps there is somewhere else nearby where we can go?"

"Well there is Palomino Corral not far from here but the horses tend to be a bit trail weary."

"Never mind that we should organise to go one day, maybe you could show me a thing or two."

Well at least she wasn't shy I thought to myself. I invited her up the next afternoon suggesting she could help me with my chores. She readily agreed.

Dad had been riding horses since he was a boy and it was because of horse that he and mother met as well. Grandfather was in the business of breeding horses and owned a large stud farm and riding school in Berkshire and we would often go over there and spend the weekend with him. The property was huge and riding about in the back fields by myself it was easy to image you were the only person in the entire world. I lost track of the times the story was recounted about the first day my father saw my mother as she mounted up on old Hassey for her first lesson. Despite living in

11

the same village they'd never met and Grandfather revelled in the detail of how father had stood opened mouth mumbling: 'exactly who is that beautiful specimen?' He was complete smitten. Grandfather expelled a great deal of effort making sure they could see each other, something he never lets my father forget. Grand mama, it would seem, didn't approve of her only daughter seeing the son of a horse trader as she put it. Eventually though she relented and father would ride five miles every day after finishing in the stables to see her. Mother still complains he used to smell when he arrived. They eventually married after he graduated from Cambridge and the rest, as they say, is history.

When they built their first home he insisted it should have a stable nearby so they could keep horses and over the years always kept two around to ride. Then on their tenth wedding anniversary Grandfather had given them each a Cleveland Bay, Allie and Ross, and like mother and father they were the perfect couple. Each standing fourteen hands high they were beautiful specimen and watching them run and play used to literally take your breath away. Evenings were spent brushing, feeding and watering them and it soon became quite a regular thing for Heide to come up and help. One evening Dad had had to stay late at work so in his absence it was my responsibility to make sure the horses were bedded down for the night. About eight Heide arrived at the backdoor as usual wondering whether I was ready to go. As we walked across to the field to find the horses the sun was just beginning to set.

We eventually saw the horses down the back and began walking towards them.

"They look so peaceful down there feeding, it seems such a shame to spoil their peace and make they come with us." She spoke so softly it was like she was talking to herself.

Despite having heard every word I said "What?"

"Come with us, it seems such a shame to disturb them."

"I know but we have to get them in before it gets dark otherwise there will be hell to pay for when Dad gets home."

"I know but look at them they seem so in love standing down there together."

I glanced over at her but she was not paying any attention to me she was too busy studying the horses below. As we got closer Heide stopped short and began to point.

"Look at his dick its enormous!"

Sure enough it was, pink and extended it almost touched the ground, it was something to behold all right. Heide began to run and I followed close behind. We were up wind and she dropped down in the long grass before they could sense we were there. I lay down beside her and we both watched as Ross began walking around Allie nudging her with his nose as she ate and tried to ignore him. Finally he trumpeted his arrival and reared up placing his front legs gently down on Allie's back. With some swinging and jostling his dick seemed to raise itself up and begin to slide its way into her bum. As we lay there and watched I slowly turned to Heide to see her reaction. She had one hand up at her mouth slowly circling her lips while she appeared to be laying on the other, the outline of her buttocks slowly rising and falling.

"It looks just like Kate explained it."

"Yes I know can you imagine what such a wondrous thing would feel like up inside you? It must feel like you're completely filled up. Look at her she's just standing there taking it all."

By this time my face was beginning to go slightly red but before I knew what was happening Heide grabbed my hand and began dragging me towards the bails of hay which stood off to one side in a derelict shed.

"What do you think your doing? I said, stumbling over the broken ground and horse shit, "that shed is a death trap there is no way I am going in there!"

She shot me a glance and said with out breathing: "I want to know how that feels and you are going to help me," tightening the grip on my hand.

Before I knew it we were climbing up the bails to the top where she suddenly flopped down all out of breath.

She closed her eyes and began to explain.

"Every night I lay in bed waiting for sleep to come, sometimes it's almost immediate but more often than not as I toss and turn I begin to get this burning sensation between my legs particularly on really hot and humid nights. No matter which way I twist and turn in the bed, no matter how much I rub or scratch my arms and legs I can never seem to make it go away. Then the other night, quite by accident, I took my softball bat to bed with me. You see we had the area finals the next day and

I wanted to make sure I batted well so I thought if I took my bat to bed with me it would bring me luck. As I lay there holding the bat to my chest the end came to rest between my legs. I turned on my side to try and get to sleep and the end came into contact with my crotch. It was the first time I had felt any relief from that feeling. The more I rubbed the bat up and down the better it felt. Over the next couple of weeks I tried all sorts of things to recreate that feeling and I have to admit that rubbing the handle of my hair brush between my legs when I'm in the bath is about as good as it gets."

I stood there with and a growing tingling sensation of my own starting in my pants. But what the hell was she talking about? Suddenly she grabbed my hand and pulled me down beside her.

"Now," she said, "I know exactly where it is you need to touch me to make me feel good and I am going to show you."

With that she slipped her shorts off and stood up in front of me with her legs slightly apart. Ah, I thought, at least I've been here before.

Pointing to the top of her crack she said, "Rub me up and down here but not too hard at first."

I began to feel extremely uneasy about this whole situation but not wanting to look as if I was scared I slowly bought my finger up to within an inch of her privates.

"Well go on," she cried, "get on with it!"

Her outburst made me jump such that my hand jerked forward and came in contact with her skin. Well it didn't feel so bad after all, it fact it felt rather warm. As I began this up and down rubbing motion she again closed her eyes and slowly let her head fall backwards. I concentrated on this action all the while watching the smile grow on her face and trying to see up between her legs.

"There just there, no a little higher there that's it keep doing that, a little harder. Perfect!"

After a while she seemed to calm down a bit and lay down beside where I was kneeling. She instructed me to slowly slide my finger down until I felt it beginning to go inside her.

"Go on, just follow the line down and you'll feel it just slip inside me, don't be afraid, I really want you to do this for me."

"I'm not afraid!" I was but I wasn't going to admit it.

"Yer well by the look on your face you've just seen a ghost. That's it push it in, now pull it out and push it in again. Perfect. Now try and get two fingers in, that's it, keep doing that until I tell you to stop."

Well I could follow instructions as good as the next guy so I did as I was told. This, I thought, must be what I'd heard referred to as fingering.

"So I'm fingering you," I ventured, a shape yes came back in reply.

"Your finger fucking me and it feels great! Now shut up and get on with it. Come on do it a bit harder and stick your thumb up a bit higher at the same time, yes that's it, now you've got it. For Christ's sake don't stop!"

We eventually tumbled out of the hay only to realise it was quite dark by now and the horses were still not in. She left me to it saying her mother was expecting her home ages ago. (Ever noticed they're never around when you want them?) It was with much effort that I finally managed to round the horses up and make up their feed for the night. By the time I got home Dad was sitting in the kitchen having his dinner. He fixed me with a particularly puzzled expression as I began to explain why I had been out so long. As I began to regale them with my tale about how the horses had been determined not to come in and how Heide and I had had to chase them clear across the county his expression changed from puzzlement to what I interrupted as slight amusement and this made me even more uneasy. Could he have guessed what I had really been doing or was it just my guilty conscious giving all my secrets away again. I decided not to wait around and find out choosing bed as the preferred option. As you might have suspected it took a long time to fall asleep that night. Finally I had managed to touch a girl but how exactly did that fit into the grand scheme of things, it was certainly enjoyable enough but was that all this sex thing was about?

I didn't see Heide for a couple of weeks but when she turned up at the backdoor one night wondering if I was ready to sort the horses out she acted as if she had been there every night for the past fortnight. Now this is typical feminine behaviour. The moment you share an intimate moment with them you don't see them for dust then all of a sudden their back as if nothing had happened and wondering why you're playing it cool.

"I'm sorry I haven't been around for the last couple of weeks but there has been some trouble at home and I wasn't allowed out."

"What sort of trouble?"

"My father has been screwing his secretary and my mother just threw him out."

"I'm sorry."

"No don't be sorry he was a complete bastard anyway."

"You can't say that about your father."

"Yes I can he was a complete bastard and I never want to see him ever again."

That night after we had attended to the horses she made me feel her up again and tell her what a naughty girl she was and how her parents didn't love her any more.

Dad had been working really hard lately, much to my mothers disgust. One night just after Easter he announced over dinner that he'd finally negotiated the deal he'd been working on for months and we were to move in the New Year. Heide was prophetic about it telling me how many new friends I'd meet and how lucky I was to be able to take the horses with me. She decided that we should part with a bang and that afternoon we met up at the stables, she wanted to ride Allie. I led the horse up to the railings that ran along the front and held Allie's head as she climbed on. I gave her the reins, jumped out of the way and off she took across the field riding bareback. That afternoon I discovered Heide really could ride a horse as she dashed up and down jumping some of the obstacles as she went. Eventually she rode back and leap off, throwing her arms around me.

"I feel wonderful and exhausted thank you for being my special friend."

It's funny really because I don't think she ever really thought of me as being particularly special, I just happened to run into her that day, my Dad just happened to have horses and I was convenient. Even so she taught me a great deal and I will never forget that first night in the haystack.

Lynn and Katrina

And where the little flowers of her breast
Just break into their milky blossoming...
Oscar Wilde

No sooner had school finished for the summer than packing began. When you've lived somewhere all your life and haven't really known any other place I couldn't help but feel uneasy about moving. I think it also had something to do with being able to pack all my possessions into half a dozen cardboard packing cases and then having to sleep in my room without any of my stuff around me. I concluded that your stuff must collect and adsorb all the bad vibes and amplify all the goods ones. It was a deeply disturbing week. I had absolutely no idea were we were moving to or where we were going to live. It was all right for Mum and Dad they'd been out and chosen the house and knew exactly where they were going but me I had had to stay with Aunt Geraldine.

She was not actually my aunt she was really someone my mother had gone to school with and I just called her aunt. I think the best part about staying there was definitely the sea. They lived just one street back from the ocean and it would take me all of five minutes to get dressed, grab my towel and be on the beach. There is something mystical about lying on a beach, listening to the waves early in the morning. Of course it would have been better if I had been lying on a deserted beach but Aunt Geraldine had a daughter my age and somehow she never failed to hear me heading out the front door, no matter how quite I was. Now you would imagine that I would've been please to have some female company on my morning beach trips but unfortunately Catherine was fat and fat girls have never done anything for me. Plump I could handle but fat never and what made it ten times worse was she fancied me like crazy and would take every opportunity given to try and kiss me. Now I had been kissed by my mother, kissed by my grandmother, kissed by more aunts and cousins than I cared to remember but I was buggered if I was going to live with the thought that Catherine was the first real girl to kiss me that I wasn't related to. So I spent what seemed like endless days avoiding lip contact and considering her enormous bulk that was no easy task. Still sitting on the beach had its upside. While I threw ball for Catherine to fetch, which she did like a good big girl, I had time to take in some of the beautiful young bodies wandering by. Occasionally I even got a wave and a smile which always made my day. Unfortunately after about a week of ball throwing and fetching Catherine finally caught on that no matter how many times she fetched the ball I was not going to let her kiss me. Thank goodness Mum and Dad found the house.

The move actually went much better than I expected. The house was even bigger than our last one and not only did I have my own bedroom I had my own bathroom as well, we had finally arrived. That first afternoon after hurriedly unpacking my stuff it was time to get out there and explore. I headed down the road not really knowing were I was going but in search of the local playground. You could always judge an area by the quality of its playground equipment. Turning right at the bottom of the street I headed up the hill and as I came to the top there it was, the best adventure playground I had ever seen. What my parents had neglected to tell me was that, not only had we moved house, we had also skipped a few rungs on the old social ladder and had managed to move into a very respectable middle class part of town. As I approached I spotted two of the most gorgeous looking girls I had ever seen seated on the swings. I decided that discretion was the better part of valour and carefully studied my trainers as I walked past.

"Hey you" I lifted my head, "Yer you what's your name?

I considered my options. Ignore them and keep on walking or acknowledge them and find out who these fine girls were. I looked over.

"Charles," I replied.

"You must be new around here we haven't seen you before."

"Yes we just moved into Haley House."

"Oh really. Well my name is Lynn and this is Katrina."

Lynn sat on the left and had long dark hair which fell over her shoulders while Katrina had light brown hair tied back in a ponytail. I walked over and stood in front of them.

"We need someone to give us a push. Think you're up to it?"

"I think so, who's first?"

"I am of course," replied Lynn.

I walked around behind the swing, placed my hands lightly on her waist and began to push.

"Harder," she cried, "I'm going for the horizontal."

I pushed harder until eventually she was almost coming off the seat as the chains indeed were virtually horizontal with the ground. By now I felt it was Katrina's turn so in between pushing Lynn I began to push Katrina as well. After about 10 minutes of this the girls were giggling and laughing and I was ready to die from exhaustion. I collapsed on the grass behind them and watched the swings die down. Lynn was the first to jump off and came over and sat down beside me. Katrina waited until her swing had almost completely stopped before she got off and did the same.

"Hey your pretty good at that you must have had some practice." Lynn looked at me with her head slightly cocked to one side and a comical expression of enquiry on her face.

"Well I guess I have, never really thought about it all that much.

"I think we're going to be great friends."

"How's that then?"

"We're your next door neighbours, I live up the lane from you and Katrina here lives a little way further down from your house."

Sounds like I got off the bus in heaven I thought to myself.

It turned out this was absolutely true. I walked home with my new neighbours and proudly introduced them to my parents. Mum glanced over at Dad with at slightly worried look on her face then just as quickly looked back at me and the girls.

"Well it's very nice to meet you I hope you will look after my little boy since he doesn't know anyone around here yet."

"Of course we will," replied Lynn with the beginnings of a smirk on her face.

It turned out Lynn and Katrina were not my only two female neighbours Michelle lived directly opposite. By the time we moved in Michele was in the fourth form and seemed completely untouchable to me. She was going out with Lynn's older brother David and I often saw them kissing against the hedge which separated our houses.

Lynn and Michelle were great friends and it was through her that I finally got the opportunity to meet Michelle. She was so cool. We used to go over there on Wednesday afternoon's when David was playing cricket and go swimming. I think it was the first time I had ever watched anyone smoke a cigarette really closely before and Michelle seemed to have this very sexy way of placing it between her lips and drawing back the smoke until the tip glowed bright red then forming an O-shape with her mouth and blowing smoke rings.

She caught me staring one afternoon, smiled and said; "Would you like a drag then?" and offered me the cigarette.

I couldn't exactly refuse so I took it from her, put it up to my mouth, and breathed in. I have never coughed so much in all my life.

Lynn grabbed it and inhaled deeply. "Here this is how you do it," exhaling the smoke in a long straight plumb. There is something very attractive about watching young girls smoke.

These Wednesday afternoon sessions went on all that summer and by the end I had learnt quite a lot. I think Lynn must have had a thing about Michelle's breasts, jealousy or something, because our swimming sessions invariably end up with Lynn undoing Michelle's top and letting her tits out for everyone to see. Apart form the lack of participation I didn't mind a bit because they were the first real breasts I had even seen. Although they weren't large they stood up proud, her dark brown nipples in stark contrast to her white breasts. Katrina never joined in these sessions instead preferring to stand back and watch. I will never be sure there wasn't something more between these two beyond the removing of bikini tops. They seemed to revel in reminding us of the fact that they often took naked midnight swims together when Lynn stayed over. In fact thinking back they seemed to spend a great deal of time together considering their age difference and I wouldn't be surprised if Michelle didn't teach Lynn a thing or two during those midnight swims. I guess it's all part of the learning process.

By the time we were ready to start back at school Lynn had started to develop a healthy pair of breasts of own and never missed an opportunity to show them off. Bitterly resisting all her mothers attempt to make her 'more respectable' as she put it,

Lynn absolutely refused to wear a bra under any circumstances. (I think it's partly for this reason that to this day I hate bras). She always used to leave the three buttons of her uniform undone at school so when she ever bent over you could see her wonderfully mysterious mounds. After school she always wore tee shirts which left nothing to the imagination and a great deal of fantasy time was spent dreaming up elaborate situations whereby she would be forced to take her top off. It only ever happened once.

Michelle and her parents had gone away for a late break and of course Lynn was asked to look after the house. One afternoon we went over there to feed the rabbit and generally check to make sure everything was in order. George, the rabbit from hell, was a right little bastard. Feeding him was fine you could usually get the door open, grab the bowl and slam it shut before he realised what was going on but cleaning the cage was a two man job. That particular afternoon I elected to block the hole off to his night hutch while Lynn did the shit scraping. I managed to get the newspaper in place over the hole before he ran out and Lynn started the disgusting task of cleaning the bottom of the cage. Why people keep rabbits I will never know all they do is eat, shit and piss and you seem to spend all your time cleaning up after them. (Almost sounds like kids really).

Anyway there I was holding the newspaper, concentrating on trying to look down Lynn's tee-shirt as she bent down, when the little shit bit me. I dropped the paper, jumped up, and started running round yelling and swearing, vowing that I was going to shoot the bloody thing. In between all the commotion George shot out of the cage and across the garden.

"Now look what you've done!"

"Hang on a minute its not my fault he bit me."

"Well if you'd been concentrating on holding the paper properly instead of trying to look down my tee shirt it wouldn't have happened.

What could I say? How had she known what I was trying to do I was always so careful?

"If anything happens to that rabbit it will be all your fault!"

Chasing a rabbit is like chasing love itself. One minute you lay your finger tips on it and you think ah ha I have you, the next second it twists and turns and you've lost it. I eventually cornered it up the back, there was no escape apart from the long narrow edge of the pool that ran alone the fence and Lynn was standing there. I approached slowly looking him straight in the eye, thinking what a wonderful stew he would make, then at the last second he shot through my legs, headed straight for Lynn down the side of the pool who panicked stumbled and fell into the pool soaking George in the process.

Until then I didn't realise how much rabbits disliked being wet, enough was enough and he just sat there dripping. I came up behind scooped him up and threw him back in the cage. Lynn had managed to get out of the pool and stood there dripping, her nipples standing straight out under her tee shirt. She looked very sorry for herself.

"My mother is going to kill me, just look, I'm soaked through." I was looking.

"Come on we'll get you dried off and I'm sure Michelle won't mind you borrowing some clothes."

I led her upstairs to the bathroom. I found the hair dryer and started drying her hair, running my hand slowly through it. We watched each other in the mirror.

She smiled, "I could used it this."

"What?"

"You looking after me."

I continued drying and then just as I finished she turned round, looked me straight in the eye and kissed me on the lips.

"I think you can have your wish now." She peeled her tee-shirt off.

"Nice aren't they?"

"Yes," I said somewhat shocked, well what are you supposed to say, no?

She walked out of the bathroom heading for Michelle bedroom and I followed. I stood in the doorway and watched while she took off her jeans and began looking through the wardrobe for something to wear. She stood choosing, trying to decide what to wear, every so often standing on tip toe to look in back of the wardrobe then bending over to look in the bottom draw, making no effort at all to be modest. Her panties rode up into the crack of her bum and it all started to become a bit too much for me. As she bent down for the third time I slipped up behind her and ran my hand along her crack.

"For a minute there I thought you were someone else," she said.

"Oh yeah and who exactly were you expecting?"

"I'm not sure, enjoying yourself then?"

"Very much."

At that moment Katrina walked in the room.

"Your mother said you were here and the door was open so I just..." She stopped mid sentence when she saw us standing there.

Lynn stood and faced me, slapping me hard across the face.

"What do you think your doing," she yelled.

"Well I just thought..."

"Well you should just stop thinking."

"Oh sorry."

Katrina mumbled a quick sorry and ran from the room.

"I'd better go after her and explain," I said.

"Explain all you like but she will never believe you."

By the time I found her she was sitting in her room looking very unhappy, I could see tears in the corner of her eyes. I went and sat down beside her on the bed, putting my arm around her.

"You like her more than me don't you, you think she's prettier than me."

Her tone was sharp and almost angry.

"No," I said, "I don't."

"Well what were you doing there and Lynn only in her underwear?"

I began to explain about the rabbit and how he had escaped, Lynn falling in the pool, and how she was just getting some dry clothes so she wouldn't get into trouble. I left out the bit about the kiss.

"I know what boys want it's all about sex, there's no room for love in relationships anywhere. If anyone should know I do."

"What the hell are you talking about? This had nothing to do with sex. OK Lynn is attractive but you, you have so much more."

"Don't treat me like I'm stupid because I'm not. I know you like her because she smells of sex, I can smell her too."

"Katrina, Lynn means nothing to me, I have always liked you better." Eventually after much persuasion she began to calm down.

After that day we decided not to see so much of Lynn, of course we still saw her at school and occasionally hung out at lunch time but that was about it. Katrina and I had begun to spend most of our time together. Katrina's mother had died the year before from Golden Staff which she contracted in hospital while having an operation on her spine so she was able to do pretty much as she pleased. She was a great roller skater and we used to go skating in London on Saturdays. I have never been all that co-ordinated but I really surprised myself how quickly I picked it up. Of course I was never up to Katrina's standard. She used to skate backwards in front of me holding my hands, leading me round the floor. (Skating was one thing but backwards with little wheels strapped to you feet not likely). She seemed to take on a new air of confidence when she put on those skates, it was as if for that short period of time she was just as good or even better than everyone else and it showed in the way she smiled and her cheeks glowed. She still missed her mother terribly and I think this affected her self-a-steam more than anything, no doubt though it also had something to do with Lynn.

Lynn was the first none relative to kiss me but it was with Katrina that I had my first real passionate kiss. As a group we often went down to the local cemetery on Friday night to smoke cigarettes and tell ghost stories. The atmosphere was somewhat less scary than you would imagine as there was always two or three other gangs of kids roaming around. One Friday night all our friends decided to go to the movies but Katrina and I had seen this particular film during the week and, as it was not exactly memorable, we decided to stay home instead. As we sat watching television we decided that a walk down to the cemetery was in order. As we walked down the street to the cemetery the wind blew softly in the trees that lined the street. Every so often a gust would make a little howling sounds in the autumn leaves. Katrina took my hand. This was something she did very infrequently however I'd noticed lately that it was happening more and more.

"Are you all right?"

"Yes, I don't care very much for the sound the wind makes when it blows hard."

We sat down the back where the action was less fraught and talked, watching the moon rise.

"I wonder what it would be like to live on the moon, just the two of us," she said.

"Boring I guess, its nothing but dust and rocks."

As I lay back she leaned over kissed me. I put my arms around her and drew her close. We kissed each other deeply allowing our tongues to explore each other's mouths.

"Do you love me?" she asked, pulling away slightly so she could see my expression.

"I don't know I've never really thought about it much." This was the wrong answer.

"Well I don't see how you can lie there and kiss me like that and have no feelings for me what so ever."

"It's not that I don't feel something for you its just..."

"Oh forget it, just take me home." Shit. Someone should write a handbook on the right answers to these questions.

Katrina had a step brother Michael who, from all accounts, used to be a really nice guy. Did well at school, had plenty of friends and had even made the school first eleven cricket team. But by the time we were introduced he was rapidly going down hill. Having failed to pass any of his GCSE's the year before he had dropped out of school and his days consisted of getting up around lunch time, going to the shops to meet his mates, pooling his money with them to buy beer and whiskey then heading back to Michael's place to get pissed. By the time we got home from school there would be a dozen or so bodies lying around the pool, all of them pissed out of their heads. The upside of this was they were always very generous with their beer and Katrina and I always managed to scam a drink or two off them. What never ceased to amaze me was that despite never appearing to be all that clean they always seemed to have plenty of girls hanging around. Jodie was my favourite. Although she was still at school she was Michael's girlfriend and used to walk home with us sometimes. Looking out my window one night I saw Michael come out and sit in their drive. Jodie was not far behind and as she approached Michael I couldn't believe my eyes as she reached under her skirt, pulled of her panties and flung them into the bushes. She came up to Michael, stood in front of him and then sat down in his lap. After some fumbling her movements became slow and deliberate and it was obvious, even from where I was watching, what they were doing. She did have a bit of a reputation around school and maybe that's why I liked her. According to the gossip she had lost her virginity to her 45 year old next door neighbour at the age of 11 and had had her first abortion at the age of 12, curiosity of the same. But the best story I ever heard was how after one particularly heavy drinking sessions up in the woods she had arranged 12 boys in a circle then stood in the middle, pealed off her jeans and one by one went round to each of them, sucked them off and sat on their dicks and fucked them until they came. Fact or fiction who knows but I do remember watching her being fingered in front of about thirty people as we lined up for Science on day. If it was fiction I would say it wasn't far from the truth. Of course this was not the best environment for Katrina to be growing up in but at least it meant she wasn't easily shocked.

Katrina usually had softball practice Tuesday afternoons so if I didn't stay and watch the team run around in their sports skirts I'd head home by myself and go round there just after she got home. One Tuesday I went round about four thirty, Michael and his mates were sitting watching a video.

"Is Katrina home yet?" I asked.

"Yes she's up stairs having a shower," replied one of his mates.

I walked up the stairs, her bedroom door was open so I went straight in. The bathroom door was also open so I stuck my head round the door. She was still in the shower.

"Would you like me to wash your back for you?" I asked.

"Come in, come in, I'm still in the shower," came the reply.

I opened the shower cubicle door, she had her back to me.

"It's unlike you to come back for a second time," she said sticking her bum out towards me.

"What are you talking about, a second time?" I asked. She turned around with a somewhat shocked look on her face.

"I thought you were Grant!"

It turns out that while I had been keeping my distance from her trying to behave myself Michael's friend Grant had spent the last six months paying her very close attention indeed. It was all too much for me. Why had I been so stupid? What on earth had made me think that Katrina was too venerable to try anything on with. What had I missed out on? It was a hard lesson to learn but one I remember well.

Elley

And finding her beauty such power has got,
Her heart pants for something, she cannot tell what.

W.B.Yeats

Seeing Katrina like that had been somewhat of a shock and I noticed walking home that my dick had gone very hard. This was still somewhat of a mystery to me. I mean I had been around animals all my life and had watched what happened when they became sexually aroused so it wasn't that I was unfamiliar with what it meant it was just that after it all died down I was always left with a very uncomfortable feeling that stayed with me for some time. I had heard my friends making jokes about masturbation, my God everyone was a wanker. And although I had the hand movements down pat it seemed as if I still didn't have the full picture. I decided that some research was in order.

My friend Jason had recently discovered his Dad's collection of girly magazines. Ever since then he had been talking about this picture and that so I thought this was as good a place to start as any. I arranged to go round to Jason's place and stay over that Friday night. His parents were going to some charity ball and wouldn't be home until really late so it looked like all was in place for a good night of research. Friday afternoon Jason told me that Elley was also coming over. This was not good news. How was I going to look through all those magazines with a girl there?

By the time I arrived Jason was already installed in his bedroom with a stack of magazines a foot high on the floor.

"See I told you unbelievable isn't it? Here look at these ones."

Well I had never seen anything like this before in my life. The first magazine I picked up had pages full of women with the biggest tits I have ever seen, I mean they were huge. (I had been down at the beach with Catherine one morning and saw this women walk past with breasts falling out of this tiny bikini top and remember thinking you could get lost in there but she had had pimples compared to these women). The next one seemed to contain pictures of peoples wives and girlfriends and although the poses were rather exciting the majority of them were old and very plain and it really did nothing for me at all. I decided to be a little more selective next time and went over and started looking through the pile. About half way down I came to a group which were all about school girls. Now we are getting somewhere. I started looking through these and was pleasantly surprised to find pictures of young girls in school uniforms having sex with men and each other. I imagined Lynn and Michelle exploring each other in the pool. I wondered why Jason's father had magazines about school girls in his collection.

Just then there was a knock on the door.

"That must be Elley," Jason said.

"What should we do with these? I asked.

"Oh don't worry about that she won't mind a bit." I wasn't at all sure.

While Jason went to get the door I got up pushed, the stack of magazines down to the end of the bed, and then sat down and tried to look as if nothing was going on. Elley was in the same class as we were and although she was not what you would describe as a classic beauty she always wore really short dresses and was very popular. Jason had been going out with her for about two weeks now, which was a new record for Jason, and they seemed like a good couple. Elley walked into the room with Jason following rapidly behind. She stood there smiling, slowly surveying the room with her eyes.

"I knew something was going on Jason Downs when you said nothing was and I'm surprised at you Charles I didn't think you were that sort of boy. So come on then which ones were you looking at then?" She headed straight for the stack of magazines.

Even from a young age women have an amazing ability to make you feel about an inch tall, cheap and dirty all with only one sentence. Then take that situation, turn it on its head and expect you to cope.

"I need a drink," I said and heading off to the kitchen to find some Coke.

I decided to leave them to it for a while and settled down to watch some television. About an hour later I was starting to get hungry so decided to find out what we were going to do about food. As I walked up the hall to Jason's bedroom I could hear all this moaning. I approached the door very quietly and poked my head round the door. Elley was sitting on the bed next to Jason, he had his trousers round his ankles and Elley had his her hand wrapped round his dick and was rubbing it up and down. He just sat there moaning with his right hand buried between her legs.

"Faster," he said.

All of a sudden a arc of fluid shot from his dick.

"There," she said, "that's much better."

I headed back to the sitting room. There was no need to study those magazines any further it was all crystal clear now.

That weekend I think I spent more time in the bathroom than anywhere else. The first time I came I felt the most wonderful sense of relief followed immediately by extreme feelings of guilt. What if someone walked in and discovered me? What if Mother guessed what I was going? What if she found out and told someone and it got all round the school? What if it fell off? It took some time but eventually I got over these worries of course, despite having been told from an early age that if I didn't leave myself alone it would fall off. It took some years though to realise that girls, as much, if not more, enjoy the art of self-pleasuring. The story I had heard from Heide was only one example. In fact Lynn used to spend long periods of time sitting on the playground fence swinging her legs back and forth, I didn't realise at the time but the amused expression on her face had nothing to do with my witty conversation.

Although some of my friends were paired off being part of such a large group took the pressure off not always having a girlfriend or boyfriend. When you wanted female company there was always someone you could ring up with and go out with. I guess it was especially easy for me because hanging around with mostly girls from an early age had taught me the value of being a good listener. Girls more than boys needed someone to share their problems with and if you could sit there and at least look as if you were interested you had a huge head start over the others. But there was a down side to this I didn't understand until many years later. When girls come to you with their problems, and it was mostly about their boyfriends, they do not think of you as a potential replacement when they break up, your just there to be a shoulder to cry on. In fat it goes muxh further than that. Being so it touch with your femaine side dulls or even removes that hard edged ability simply to talk girls into going to bed with you. I believed I missed many wonderful experiences in my teenage years because I was 'such a nice guy', how I hate those particular words.

After witnessing that scene at Jason's place I decided that Elley was someone I needed to know and over time we became the best of friends. Most weekends were spent going to someone or anothers house to watch videos or listen to music. One particular Saturday night at Elley's place we were all down stairs in the games room playing pool when Elley walked in and promptly fainted under the score board. I didn't notice straight away as I was busy lining up my shot but when Suzy screamed out her name we all soon knew something was wrong. I rushed round the table to find out what was going on. I picking her head up and told everyone to stand back and give her some space. Jason appeared at the door and asked what the hell was going on. When I said she had fainted he began to look rather worried. She was only out for a minute and looked rather embarrassed when she saw everyone standing around looking at her.

"I'm fine," she said getting to her feet, "just fine."

"But you just fainted," Suzy almost screamed.

"I'm fine honestly!"

"Let me take you up to your room." I said.

I walked with to her room and I sat her down on the bed.

"Are you all right?"

"Yes I just need a drink of water." I came back with a large glass of water which she drank down in one go. "That's much better. I just lost my virginity, I guess it was all a bit much.

"So how was it?" I shouldn't have said that.

She shot me a look and said, "Yer it was all right I guess, better than I expected, I'm just glad of all those horse riding lessons."

It must have been more than all right though because Jason spent the next four weeks telling me all the places they had done it. They were like rabbits, they couldn't stop. In fact according to Elley, Jason followed her round with a perpetual hard on all the time. In her words one fuck simply blurred into the next. But she did tell me about one particular afternoon. They spent the day in the woods having sex whenever

Jason could manage the next erection. Around lunchtime they were going for it, laying in the sunshine, when Elley said she need to go for a pee and if Jason didn't stop now she would piss all over him. He said there was no way he was going to stop now and if she wanted to piss she would just have to wait till he finished. Elley didn't like the idea of anyone telling her what to do, even if it was Jason and proceeded to take a pee with his dick inside her. Far from being put off by this however Jason picked up speed and ended up having the most powerful climax of the afternoon. If this story had come from Jason it would have been almost impossible to believe, but Elley sat there and told me this with a straight face so I had no reason not to believe her.

She became rather unsettled at home for a while after that. About half way through the mid term break Dad came into my room late one night.

"There's a phone call for you."

Who would be ringing so late at night I wondered, no one ever rang after I'd gone to bed.

"It's Elley's mother," he said. I got out of bed trying to imagine what she could want so late at night.

"Hello Mrs Garson" I said rather apprehensively.

"Charles Elley's run away," she said almost hysterical. Run away I thought don't be so stupid.

"No," I said, "she's just late, she's probably round at Jason's house and they've just forgotten what time it is."

"No no you don't understand I just had a phone call from Lee's mother, she found a note on her pillow they've run away together."

Lee was Elley's best friend despite the fact they were completely different. She had started school with us but her father had decided that there were too many boys at the school (why he had not thought of that before she started I will never know) so she was due to start the new term at the Church of England girls school in the next village. Lee's father was the local vicar and they lived up the road from us in a beautiful 17th century vicarage. I'd been there a couple of times with Elley but her father was home all the time and both her parents were really strict about everything. I wasn't even allowed in Lee's bedroom! So although I knew her parents I only went round there if Elley was with me and we were on our way out somewhere else.

"Don't worry Mrs Garson I'm sure they haven't really run away, they probably haven't gone far at all you know what Elley's like."

Like me she rather enjoyed the comforts of home, her mother spoilt her rotten and I couldn't imagine she would be very far from her four poster bed. I told her again not to worry and said if I heard anything she would be the first to know and rang off. No sooner had I put down the phone than it rang again. It was Lee's father. This was turning into quite a night.

"I suppose you know then," he said in his best disapproving tone.

"Yes'" I said, not wanting to acknowledge his disapproval.

"Well where are they?"

"I have absolutely no idea."

"I told her she wasn't to see that Elley again now look what trouble she has got my daughter in." This was starting to get ugly. "If they ring tell her she had better get home immediately or I'll take my cane to her." Such love and compassion.

They had run away though. They rang me early the next morning to say they were fine and could I ring their mothers and tell them not to worry. Mrs Garson was remarkably calm considering the tone of her voice last night. Of course she was worried about where her daughter was and whether she was in any trouble but I told her they had promised to ring again tonight and I was doing everything possible to persuade them to come home. She told me to tell Elley to ring home after she had spoken to me and said she would speak to me tonight. Lee's mother did not take the news quite so well. She went absolutely ballistic. Who the hell was I to be receiving phone calls from her daughter when they were on the run and what was I going to do about the situation? Dad took the phone from me at this point and told Mrs Child in no uncertain terms that this had absolutely nothing to do with me and they had just rung me so they wouldn't have to speak to her! Good old Dad. This went on for four days. Sunday night, the day before school started, Elley and Lee turned up on our doorstep looking like they had just spent four days in a holiday resort. I have to hand it to my mother she was brilliant. She bought them both in, sat them down in the kitchen, and made tea and sandwiches for them. And although we were all dying to know where they had been she didn't ask any questions, simply served tea and then instructed my father to drive them both home. Poor old Dad looked a little worse for wear when he finally got back.

"I hope we never have to go through that again," he said heading for the conservatory and his paper.

The story unfolded bit by bit over the next few days. It seemed that when Lee's mother delivered her ultimatum Lee decided to teach her parents both a lesson and talked Elley into running away with her. They were picked up by two lads in a Mercedes and had spent four days in a hunting lodge on the Scottish border. It seems they hadn't been sleeping under the stars or eating out of rubbish bins as everyone imagined instead they had had an obsolete ball, treated like royalty as Elley described it. What else happened they remained tight lipped about and no matter how much we questioned them they were determined this was going to remain their secret. They'd only been bought home when one of the guys discovered Elley's wallet by accident with her school library card in it and they'd been forced to confess they were only fourteen. Of course the accusations continued to fly, mostly from the vicars camp, but Lee go her way at least and was able to see Elley once a month.

Angela

So soft she looked, so sweet, so fair,
With such a winning, yielding air...
William Pattison

Barry was and has remained my best friend. Like Elley and Lee though we were very different. For a start he was the only one of my friends who's parents were divorced and he lived with his mother and brother in a modest bungalow behind the school. His father, who he knew, but hardly ever saw, was an alcoholic, his mother had thrown him out when Barry was only three. She was a big woman who didn't suffer fools gladly and I think she had had a pretty hard life bringing up two boys by herself. Although she provided well for them with the business she ran I don't think they had ever had much money even when his Dad was living with them. I remember Mrs Russell telling me that when they moved into the house just after they had been married, they could only afford one light bulb and used to carry it around from one room to another in a damp hand towel. How they managed I'll never know, Dad couldn't even reach any of the light sockets in our house without climbing on a step ladder.

The three events in the school calendar we all looked forward to the most were swimming carnival, sports carnival and summer vacation. Vacation is easy to understand but carnivals usually meant doing large amounts of physical exercise which for me particularly was not my idea of fun. In fact I hated anything to do with sports especially gym. Just the thought of looking up those ropes in the gym and knowing there was no way you were ever going to reach the top was something I never looked forward to. (I went back to the school gymnasium some years later to vote for the first time and remember looking at those same ropes and thinking they must have lowered the ceiling since I'd left because they were only about twelve feet floor to ceiling, in fact everything looked so much smaller than I had remembered it. Bending down to drink from one of the water fountains was like entering another world). Those two events were different though. Primarily because you weren't stuck in some stuffy classroom learning about things which had absolutely nothing to do with real life. Or perhaps more importantly swimming carnival meant you got to stare at all the school lovely's parading around with next to nothing on without getting your face slapped and sports carnival provided the finest show of underwear anywhere in the country. Both of these events were dominated by the presence of Angela Billbury. While the girls in our form were no dragons, compared to Angela they all came a poor second. To look at her you would swear she was eighteen, solidly built yet with perfect muscle tone there was not an ounce of fat on her body. She possessed a huge pair of tits which were the envy of every girl in the form and to top it all off she was a natural athlete, one of these people that never had to train yet could out throw, out run and out jump almost anyone in the school. And how had this all come about? Her parents owned a substantial sheep holding not far from where we lived and ever since she was a little girl Angela had been helping her father on the farm.

"I think they would have preferred a boy," she had explained one day, "not that I mind helping out you understand, at least it's given me good tone."

She stood in front of us hands on hips tightening and untightening the muscles in her arms and legs, it was a sight not easily forgotten.

After a particularly memorable sports carnival this year at which she wore a tiny little blue sports skirt which barely finished below her knickers Barry and I decided that she was going to sit with us at the swimming carnival and that we would be her personal cheer leaders when she swam. Angela more than anyone loved a drink, able to consume vast quantities without seeming the least bit tipsy, it must have had something to do with all those early spring morning nips of brandy with her father as they tired to keep warm during the lambing. We corned her the day before the carnival as she headed for the bike shed.

"We've been thinking and it seems these swimming carnivals are a bit of a bore so to liven things up a bit we are designating tomorrow The Cocktail Carnival. We thought you might like to join us in the stands between events.". No doubt about Barry he had a way with words that could charm the birds out of the trees.

"That sounds great but how are you going to get anything in?"

"Don't worry leave that up to us."

"See you tomorrow then."

That night we went straight round to Barry's place to prepare the suppliers. For weeks now we had been siphoning off quantities of vodka from the drinks cabinets at home and had even managed to secure a hip flask of gin from one of the older boys at school, at quite a considerable cost I might add. We had three thermos flasks cleaned and ready for the job. No one was going to be checking thermos flasks. The plan was brilliant. We prepared the three different flasks, one vodka and orange, one martini thanks to some vermouth donated by Mrs Russell and one gin, vodka and pineapple juice mix which tasted far too good. We were all set.

The ground staff had out done themselves this year unbelievably the pool actually looked clean. It had been a source of much discussion last year when one of the girls relay teams had refused to compete because you couldn't see the bottom but this year the water looked like it had been flown in from the Mediterranean. We took our seat directly in line with the starting blocks which gave you the best view of all the girls bending over ready to jump in and waited for Angela to arrive. She walked in one of the side doors about five minutes later and immediately spotted us sitting up in the stand.

"So are we all prepared for The Cocktail Carnival then?" she said as she came up the stairs.

"I think so what about you?" Barry replied.

"Don't worry about me refreshments are in the bag. I could have done with a little more notice though."

"Yer sorry it was sort of a last minute thing."

She propped her bag up against the back of one of the seats and began to undress. Within in ten seconds she was standing there in front of us in an almost see through white one piece.

"I'm only swimming in the first event, see you in a bit," and she sprang off towards the staring blocks.

"Did you see that? I said turning to look at Barry.

"I did, told you this was a brilliant plan."

Unassuming in the way she carried herself she seemed to have no idea how attractive she really was or what effect she had on the male population of the school. She won her race to the sound of a rising ovation from the boys and came bounding back up the steps to us dripping wet. I handed her a towel and we watched as she dried herself off, nipples standing erect and a small black patch just visible above her crotch. She dropped down into her seat.

"Right then now that that's all over lets get this party on the road."

Throughout the day I think we must have been visited by almost every boy in the school, some just passing by and casually say hi while others sat down and chatted, generally talking complete bollocks. I imagine more than one couldn't help but wonder what she was doing sitting with us but that didn't matter, let them think what they like I thought, she was here and she was ours and that was something none of them could take away from us. As the day wore on we slowly got more pissed cheering loudly when ever a girls race was about to begin.

"You know you're very popular Angela you should run for school captain next year," I started, repeating a thought that had been running round in my head for some time.

"Don't be so stupid I don't go in for that sort of thing besides why would any one want to vote for me?"

"Are you kidding I don't know any one who wouldn't."

"Well with all that's going on at the farm at the moment there is no way I could spare the time, Dad needs me too much."

"We could help you couldn't we Barry?" I nudged him and he nearly fell off his seat. "For Christ's sake try and at least look like you haven't drunk an entire thermos of vodka and orange all yourself, we don't want anyone getting suspicious."

It was no good trying to get any sense out of him now so I dropped the subject. I had always been interested in politics and rather fancied myself as a campaign manager but she wasn't having any of it.

The afternoons festivities drew to a close and we decided to make a break for it with the crowd, the last thing we wanted was to be seen stumbling down the isles by Mr Sikes the sports master. Somehow we managed to make it outside in one piece, deciding that the bikes should stay where they were, and headed back to Barry's place to sober up. After what seemed like walking the London to Brighton marathon we finally stumbled through the front door and crashed out in the sitting room.

Within minutes Barry was snoring heavily and I was rapidly heading the same way when Angela suddenly lifted her head.

"Do you think I'm attractive, I mean do you think anyone could ever fancy me?"

"I think your very attractive in fact that's what most of the boys think at school."

There was silence for a while longer.

"Have you ever done it with anyone before?"

"In the classic sense of the word? No."

"I have."

"You have when?"

"Last year I went to summer camp in Sweden. The place was packed with over sexed Swedish girls looking to get their hands on anything that wasn't dead. By the time I got there though the majority of the instructors were pretty much immune to their advances, probably exhausted from a full summer of activities."

"Poor bastards, my hearts bleeding for them."

"Anyway there was one particularly good looking guy, an Italian by the name of Roberto, he used to pronounce his name by rolling the R's which would make any girl cream her pants. He was the swimming coach and since this was one of my strengths we took to swimming together early in the morning and then again late in the afternoon after all the lessons were finished. As you can probably imagine he was very smooth and blessed as he was I was soon fantasising about what it would be like to be taken by him one night by the pool and decided there and then he would be the one to make me a women. One evening after our swim I began complaining about how tight my shoulders were, half-heartedly rubbing my hands over them. He immediately volunteered to give them a massage and, crouching down behind me, he began to do just that with his big powerful hands. I became very light headed sitting there and closed my eyes, letting my mind wander. He suggested that this would work much better if the muscles are warm and suggested I should take a shower. This snapped me back to reality. Before he knew what was happening I was on my feet and dragging him off in the direction of the shower block. We went into the girls changing room and I turned on four shower heads, slowly turning round and round as the water flew in every direction. I felt him behind me. He cupped my breasts in his hands and I could feel the bulge of his manhood nudging my back. With one graceful movement he took me and we began to make love right there in the shower. I told this was my first time which seem to excite him even more. By the time we had finished it was dark outside and as we began to walk back I pushed him to the ground and rode him one last time. I had made my fantasy came true."

"That's some story I don't suppose your shoulders are feeling tense at the moment?"

"No their fine thank you, anyway I had better be getting home before my father sends out a search party. See you tomorrow and thanks for a great day."

And with that she got up and left. Angela's father died that year of a heart attack and she left school not long after the carnival to help her mother run the farm. To my knowledge she still lives there with her elderly mother and has never married.

Mandy

Her hands, her lips did love inspire,
Her every grace my heart did fire.
But most her eyes, which languish with desire.
John Dryden.

Dad was still working long hours and often came home almost too tired to eat. We didn't get to see him all that much during the week but the two things he held sacrosanct though were the weekends and our summer holiday. Each year we went through a ritual to decide where we were going. Mother passed out three pieces of identical paper, she made sure they were identical, and we each wrote down countries we would like to spend our two weeks in. We then chose one piece of paper each from the top hat she used to keep in the hall closet specifically for this purpose. Dad would then mix them up until you couldn't tell who chose which one then with all the ceremony of the town crier he'd read out the destination. If the destination he chose was the same as the year before the second one would be opened. The third one was just for luck and we rarely had to resort to opening it. Except for one year. He opened the first to find Italy had been chosen, we had been there the year before and when he opened the second one and found I had written Peru I was overruled. Well it certainly sounded like an interesting country, all those lamas roaming about and guru's living everywhere. We went to the Caribbean that year.

This year we all sat down on the last Saturday in October, it was always the same day, out came the hat and mother passed round the pieces of paper she had prepared. I scribbled down France, Italy and Spain and was the first to get my pieces of paper in the hat. We had been talking at school and decided these were the three best destinations for meeting women. As it turned out I got my way and Dad read out France, it was fate. I have always been a great believer in the fate. I truly believe that the main events in your life are pretty much pre-determined and that there is very little you can do to change them. So it was to be with France.

When I arrived at school on Monday and told Barry where we were going, there was great excitement at the prospect of meeting some lovely French girls. The shared excitement came down to the fact that since Mrs Russell ran a business of her own she rarely took time off so the possibility of going away for two weeks in the summer was almost non-existent. Therefore Barry had started to join us some years back to keep me company. Mum and Dad didn't mind because it meant they could go out for the evening without having to arrange for a baby-sitter. We had both been studying French and were coming along very nicely so we thought we at least stood a pretty good chance of chatting up some French maidens.

The months seemed to drag on through one of the coldest winters we had ever had. It was that Christmas we got snowed in, I've never seen anything like it. Four mornings in a row I had to climb out of the sitting room window and shovel the snow away from the doors just so we could get outside and by the fourth day I could climb straight from the sill on to the snow. By the time it stopped we had no electricity, no running water and the telephone lines were down. Luckily we had been warned about how bad the winters could be when we moved in and had stocks of food and bottled gas. The days were very quiet, snow has an amazing ability to absorb sound.

It was the first time I ever imagined what it would be like to be the only person left in the entire world. I imagined that aliens had come down to earth one night, vaporised almost everyone except a selection of breeding pairs which they took back to a planet close to their own to breed slaves. I had been in the bath at the time and hadn't heard the knock on the door so they had missed me. (Overly simple I know but it made sense at the time if you didn't think to much about that part). They had also missed one other person, a girl. Of course the fantasy consisted of selecting who it has you were to be left with and what would happen once you realised everyone else had gone. What would you do first? Where would you live? How would you travel to other countries, would you want to? What would happen when the power started going off and the water stopped running? What would you do for food once all the supplies were out of date? I always imagined it would be so cool to be able to go into all the houses of the girls at school and rummage around in their bedrooms discovering what sort of panties they wore. As you can appreciate the possibilities grew wider and more varied as the fantasy was given life and it ended up being a regular topic of conversation whenever the boys got together. At the time I preferred to think I had been left with Susan trying to imagine what she looked like now she was grown up. It usually ended up thinking how wonderful it would be not to have to wear any clothes and being able to see Susan naked all the time.

Summer finally arrived and we were on our way. Mum and Dad had selected a beautiful villa in a little town just outside St Tropes. We had been down to the Cote-D'Azur some years before and stayed in a hotel on the front in Cannes. I didn't remember all that much about it apart from the fact that there was a private beach for hotel guests only and you could order anything you wanted and charge it to the room which I thought was great. We flew out Saturday morning from Heathrow into Nice where we picked up our hire car. I always found it quite disconcerting driving on the wrong side of the road although Dad never seemed all that worried apart from swearing whenever he grabbed at the door to change gear. The weather was absolutely beautiful. We drove down the coast road towards Cannes and the sea was a brilliant aqua marine, sparkling in the midday sun. We stopped in Cannes for lunch at the hotel we had stayed in previously then walked along the front to the marina. I never fail to be amazed by the sight of so many beautiful craft being in one place at the same time. Thinking about all the money tied up to those jetties made my head spin. It would have been great to go on a sailing holiday one year, the only problem was Dad could get sick just looking at a boat. We didn't stay long.

The villa turned out to be better than I expected. It was situated just outside a little village in the hills above St Topes and as we drove through the village we saw an old women in black sitting in a wicker chair outside her house. She looked up as we went by and gazed at us blankly wondering I guess who we were and what we thought we were doing driving through her village. I will never forget her face, dark and foreboding, deeply lined and withered from years of sun. I couldn't help but feel that this was a place time had forgotten.

Standing on my bedroom balcony I looked down over the town with the sea beyond and wondered what all the poor people were doing today.

"It's perfect," said Barry as he walked out from his bedroom.

"Yes isn't it just," I replied. "Can't stay here all afternoon though, get changed and I'll race you to the pool, last one ins a rotten egg." We both took off, reaching the pool at virtually the same time and dove in without even testing the temperature. Luckily is was lovely and warm.

The first few days passed uneventfully with early mornings spent by the pool, lunch in town and afternoons on the beach with Mum and Dad. I was beginning to wonder whether we would ever get to meet any French girls.

Thursday afternoon we were lying on the beach watching the world go by, well actually watching the breasts go by. I thought that was one of the most wonderful things about The Continent. You spent an entire year trying to make out the shape of everyone's breasts as they go by and then for two weeks in the year you can look at the real thing to your hearts content. It almost maked up for the whole rest of the year. As we lay there on our stomachs, to avoid any embarrassment, two particularly fine specimens came walking along the waters edge. I nudged Barry to get his attention and he raised his eyebrows when he realised what I was looking at. I still find it extremely difficult to judge how old girls are when they're wearing bikinis but I figured they were about 15 and told Barry the same. As they passed in front of us they casually looked across, smiled and whispered something to each other.

"Your in my son," said Barry as they passed by.

"Don't be stupid they only smiled at us."

"Well what did you want them to do race over and grab your old boy?"

"No I just don't think you should jump to any conclusions that's all."

"Well we'll see."

A little while later we decide to call it a day and Mum and Dad headed off to get the car leaving Barry and I to gather the last of our things together. As we walked up the beach who should be sitting on the wall eating ice cream but the two girls who had passed us on the beach.

"Here we go," said Barry striding off in their direction.

Now I don't consider myself to be shy but I have always had extreme difficulty simply walking up to strangers and starting a conversation. Compared to Barry though I was a wall flower, I think he was capable of striking up a conversation with a house brick. Bold as brass he sidled up to them, introduced himself and as I came closer I heard him say and this is my very best friend Charles Wilde. You had to hand it to him.

"My name is Mandy and this is my cousin Dominique."

"Hello," said Dominique in a think French accent.

"So what brings you to France then Mandy?"

"I'm staying with Dominique for the summer, my parents are on a tour of South East Asia for a couple of months and I wasn't allowed to stay home by myself."

I stood there and listened as the two of them talked, occasionally catching Mandy's eye as she looked past Barry to where I was standing. I felt a tap on my shoulder. It was Dad.

"Come on boys the cars here, and without skipping a beat finished, "and who are these two lovely girls then?"

I blushed a little and introduced Mandy and Dominique. "This is my father."

"Very nice to meet you Mr Wilde," Mandy said extending her hand. Dad took her hand and kissed the back of it very lightly.

"Charmed I'm sure. Perhaps you two would like to come and visit on the weekend we have a lovely pool at the villa and I'm sure the boys would be thrilled."

"That sounds delightful," said Mandy, "but I have a better idea. Dominique's father owns Seville's night-club here in town and there is a big party there tomorrow night, perhaps you two would like to come along," she said indicating to us as she spoke.

"Well we were thinking of coming into town for dinner anyway so we could drop them off."

"It's settled then we'll see you tomorrow night."

As we walked towards the car I turned towards Barry and asked him whether he knew exactly what had just happened back there.

"I have no idea but I think we have a date for tomorrow night."

The next day was spent in fevered anticipation of the night ahead. I was too pre-occupied even to go to the beach that afternoon, instead I spent it in my room trying to decide what to wear. As the time to leave approached I took a long bath, washed my hair, cut and cleaned my finger nails then polished my shoes before getting dressed. Anyone who thinks that men spend little or no time thinking about their appearance and wondering what to wear has never lived in a house with a teenage boy. As I finished dressing Dad came into the room and closed the door behind him.

"I think its time we had our sex talk don't you?"

This was not good, talking about sex with your mates was one thing but hearing your father say the word made me extremely uncomfortable.

"Well I don't think this is really necessary do you I mean we've had sex education lessons at school and I think I know everything I need to know."

"That may be so but it's still my responsibility to go over the basics to make sure you don't get yourself or anyone else into trouble."

So I sat down beside him and nodded in the appropriate places as he preceded to tell me about sex.

"When girls get to a certain age they start their periods which is natures way of telling them they were able to have babies. You may find that at this particular time of the month they change into completely different beings, usually with two heads," he added. "Therefore it's best to steer clear until it is all over. If you can't I suggest you just agree with everything they say and for Christ sake don't tell them their wrong about anything. Well in fact that rule applies all the time but especially at that time of the month. Girls are completely different creatures to us they like to take things slowly at first so don't rush into anything, take your time. The actual sex act is not what it is ultimately all about, its about love and making love to someone you feel deeply about. Remember that women like you to spend time on making them feel good. Take your time, don't rush into anything otherwise you'll be disappointed."

We moved from here onto protection and without a blink of the eye he produced a packet of condoms from his trouser pocket.

"You have to wear one of these to make sure the girl doesn't get pregnant. Now I'm not giving you these and saying this is a green light for you to have sex. I am giving you these so that should you find yourself in a situation and you don't have any choice then you'll have them. Remember French girls tend to be far more advanced for their age than English girls." And with that he got up and left.

As I sat there and tried to reconcile what he had just said with what I had heard from my mates and from what I had learnt from my own limited experience I couldn't quite fit the pieces together. From what I had heard and seen it was the female who was the sexual predator and initiated most things not the other way round. Barry walked in at that moment asking whether I was ready.

"Has your mother ever given you the sex talk?" I asked.

"Of course, you can't shut her up about the subject."

"Well Dad just gave me mine."

"Shit," he said, with a worried look on his face. "Are you all right?

"Yes I think so."

We headed into town and the night-club. They dropped us off outside and said they would see us at one. We went around to the side door, rang the bell and after explaining who we were Dominique buzzed us up. Dominique stood at the top of the stairs looking absolutely radiant in a strapless black dress, her hair arranged in a dramatic swirl on the top of her head.

"Mandy will be here soon she is just getting ready no? I must apologise for my English the practice does not happen very many times. Mandy speaks very well French so there is little need for speaking English.

"We have been doing French at school but when French people French they speak very quickly and it is difficult to understand." Barry, always the charmer.

As they stood talking Mandy entered the room. She was more beautiful than I remembered. She wore a white dress with little straps and a stunning string of pearls round her neck. Her eyes seemed to sparkle under the lights as she walked towards us.

"You look wonderful, I said. "That dress really suits you."

"Thank you, you look pretty handsome yourself. I love the waistcoat, is it Boss?"

"Yes, how did you know?

"My father is in the ready-to-wear business, that's all we talk about at home." She turned her attention to the others.

"Doesn't Dominique look stunning in that dress? We bought it this afternoon in a little place just across the road from the beach." She turned back to look at me.

"Your father is certainly a charmer isn't he, he has a real way with the women, I bet your mother has to keep him on a short lead." I had never really thought about it but I guess he was. Like father like son.

Before I had time to pursue that thought any further Dominique's father came in dressed in a tuxedo and introduced himself.

"Welcome to the Club Servile I am glad you are here to look after my girls, I'm sure you will behave yourselves and remember Dominique if you are drinking downstairs you will be going straight to bed without arguing. I wish I could stay and talk longer but I have things to attend to."

When he had gone Dominique bought out a bottle of red wine and poured us all a glass.

Barry proposed a toast. "Viva le France!"

We stayed drinking until about eleven by which time Barry and I were starting to feel somewhat light headed. I wished I had had more than just a snack before we left. Before we went downstairs to the club the girls excused themselves and went to the bathroom. It is an amazing phenomenon really how you can travel the world and two things never change. McDonald's and the inability of women to go to the toilet by themselves. I've often wondered what happens, you know, does one stand there and listen while the other pees or what. While they were away we decided who was going to have whom. Barry was more than happy with Dominique, as she was French he thought he had more of a chance. I on the other hand preferred Mandy, there was something indefinably wonderful about the way she looked at me with those eyes that made my heart melt.

They returned refreshed and as Barry took Dominique's arm I took Mandy's and we proceeded downstairs. By the time we got there the place had begun to fill up. Dominique took as round, introducing us first to the DJ's who were two Afro-Caribbean chaps with the most amazing dreadlocks and then the head barman. Exactly what she said to him I couldn't be sure because of the music and the fact that I can't lip read French. The barman leaned across and kissed her fully on the mouth which surprised me but surprised Barry even more.

"Don't worry," she said later, "I allow him to pay me some attention and that way I get all the drinks I want."

It was time to get on with some serious dancing. Now I considered myself to be a reasonable dancer although when we reached the dance floor Mandy soon showed me that she had had a little more practice than I and took control of the situation. We danced as the time passed quickly, every so often catching sight of Barry and Dominique across the floor. As half past twelve rolled around we headed for the couches in the attie room.

"That was really great I don't think I have ever been to a real night club before."

"Oh I have. When my parents are away my older sister dresses me up and we go out in London, she knows all the best places and has lots of friends all over. She says she would rather have me with her where she can keep an eye on me than at home doing God knows what."

"You live in London then?"

"Yes most of the time. We have our London home in Richmond on the river and I go to Richmond Girls. It a beautiful place have you ever been there?"

"Yes we were there for dinner last year at a client's of my fathers."

"We also have a country house in a little village outside Oxford, I hope to be going to university there when I finish."

"Oh really what are you planning to do?"

"I'm not sure but I rather fancy reading English, what I will do afterwards I don't know. But that's enough about me where are you from?"

"Oh no I like listening to you talk."

"No tell me about yourself."

"Well I was born in Cambridge but we live in Hertford now, my father moved the head office of the company he owns down there some years ago. It's not as pretty as Cambridge or Oxford but I do like living in a smaller town, at least you get to recognise people on the street. I would like to go back to Cambridge though for university, I hope to do engineering."

"Engineering?"

"Yes my fathers company is an engineering company and I am expected to take it over one day so doing engineering seems to make sense." She didn't really seem to be listening to me all that intently, instead she seemed to be studying the expressions on my face. We sat there without saying anything simply looking at each other, she had beautiful high cheek bones and perfect baby-like skin. I leaned over and kissed her. She smelt wonderful.

"It's time to go your parents will be waiting." Barry was standing over us with Dominique on his arm, she smiled knowingly at Mandy.

They walked us out to the door. "So shall we see you tomorrow?" Mandy asked

"If you like." I said not trying to give away the fact that it was an absolute must.

"Why don't you come up to the villa for lunch?"

"Sounds great." We kissed once more and said goodnight.

In the car on the way home all I could see was her face as she sat there on the couch. On the steps Barry stopped me. "So how did you get on then?"

"Fine, all I remember is she smelt like heaven."

"Yer so did Dominique, we owe your father big time."

"I know, I just can't wait for tomorrow."

That night I feel asleep thinking of Mandy and dreamt extensively. We were married and she was pregnant with our second child. We living in a resplendent Victorian manor house in Devon. (Don't ask me why I remember it was Devon, maybe it had something to do with the fact that my grandparents lived in a similar house down there). I watched her through the kitchen window as she walked across the lawn in a transparent white dress and thought what a lucky man I was. I woke early the next morning with an unexplained feeling of contentment, the day was full of promise. I went for a walk by myself before breakfast in the hills above the villa and sat watching the insects going about their early morning business before the sun got too hot. What was going to go wrong? Shit, where had that thought come from? Why was it when you were on top of the world thoughts like that could come and invade your inner peace? Nothing was going to go wrong, the girls would arrive around lunch time, we would swim in the afternoon and then see what happened.

I walked slowly back to the villa tossing these thoughts over in my mind. The cook had arrived by the time I got back but no one else was up yet. She was a huge women who always seemed to have a smile and would laugh at the most unexpected times. She spoke what could best be described as very broken English. Between her poor English and my French however I had determined her children were all grown up and moved away and she took this job because it was close to the village and she had an excuse to spend time away from her husband who had recently retired. The croissants had just come out of the oven which was always the best time to eat them.

"I think you like these hotted Master Wilde," she said as she waved the tray under my nose.

"Yes that will be just fine." I spread two with fresh butter and home made strawberry jam, this was about as good as breakfast got. Although I was still getting used to how strong she made the coffee I accepted one all the same and headed for the breakfast table which had been set by the pool. Eventually the rest of the family joined me by which time I was almost bouncing off the walls from all the caffeine.

"Your mother and I are going to the Casino in Monte Carlo and we'll be staying at the hotel tonight. Do you think you two can be trusted enough to stay here by yourselves or should I have Marie stay here with you?" Barry and exchanged a knowing glance.

"Of course you can don't worry about us, we're old enough to look after ourselves. Oh by the way Mandy and Dominique are coming for lunch today and we're going to swim in the pool so there is no need to go to the beach this afternoon. I have already told cook we will be home for lunch today and she is preparing something special.

"Well that's fine by me I'd rather relax if we are going to the casino tonight anyway," mother relied absently.

"Come on Barry I've been sitting here long enough waiting for you to drag your lazy bones out of bed, we have things to do." We left them reading the morning papers and headed for the cellar.

"What do you think our chances are our getting the girls to stay over tonight?" I asked, the thought having already passed unspoken between us.

"Well if we play our cards right I think our chances are better than even, why don't you ring and explain the situation to Mandy, if I tried explaining it to Dominique I could be an old man before I finished."

"OK but before we go what do you know about wine?"

"Nothing why?"

"Well it seems to me that if they are coming up here tonight we had better be prepared."

"Well why don't you ask Marie, she seems to know everything."

"Good idea. I'll meet you by the pool in half an hour." I walked back to the kitchen trying to think how I was going to explain this to Marie, I decided on the direct approach since during the translation the subtlety would be lost.

"So what's for lunch then?

"Ah you will be waiting to see."

"Oh just a hint."

"What?"

"A clue something so I can guess what it is."

"No you must be watching." I think she meant waiting but I wasn't going to argue.

How was I going to start this? "You know Mr and Mrs Wilde are going to the casino tonight don't you?"

"Yes Mrs Wilde was telling me this at the breakfast"

"Well as you know the two girls we met yesterday are coming to the villa today and I would like them to stay for dinner. What about making your special pepper steak?"

"The special pepper steak no problem for Master Wilde.

"The only problem is I don't know what wine to serve with it, can you select something from the cellar?"

"You will be leaving this to me I am fixing everything." Well that went better than I thought it would no discussion about how we were too young to be drinking, still the French had a very different attitude to these sort of things. It was more important that the wine was right rather than how old the drinkers were.

I went back to find Barry. "We're all set, Marie is making her pepper steak tonight for four and she's going to select the wine."

"Well I don't see we can go wrong. Have you rang Mandy yet?"

"No," I said defensively, "I've been talking to Marie I can't do two things at once."

Actually I was rather nervous about ringing Mandy and decided a bath was in order first. I lay there going over the conversation in my mind. Well its just that my parents are going to the casino tonight and they won't be here to take you back to town tonight. I dried myself, dressed and heading for the phone, I had better get it over and done with. Just as I was about to pick up the receiver there was a knock at the door. I opened it and there stood Mandy and Dominique.

"When you said come for lunch we didn't know whether you meant English lunch or French lunch so we decided to hedge our bets and come early, I hope you don't mind."

"No, no. of course come in. I think Barry is out by the pool."

"The girls are here, they weren't sure whether we meant French or English lunch so they decided to come early."

"Oh fine, come and make yourselves comfortable."

Mother walked out and introduced herself.

"Hello I'm Mrs Wilde and you must be the girls I have been hearing so much about." You had to love her.

"All good I hope," said Mandy, glancing at me as if for confirmation.

"Of course," I said. "Would you expect anything else?" There was no reply only a look as if to say I should hope not.

We spent the afternoon by the pool soaking up the sun. The girls wore matching white bikini's which contrasted their deep tans dramatically. As the afternoon drew to a close Mandy and I went for a walk in the hills.

"I have something to tell you."

"What?" she was watching me wondering what was coming next.

"Mum and Dad are going to the casino in Monte Carlo tonight and won't be around to take you home. Do you think Dominique's father would come up after the club closes?"

"Well as a matter of fact he is not exactly expecting us home tonight," she said with a smile growing on her face.

"What do you mean?"

"Well we have already told him we would be staying here tonight, it would be a same to disturb him now, I'm sure he has more important things to worry about.

She raised her head and looked me squarely in the eye. "I'm sure we can trust you, no need to spoil your parents night out either."

"Yes I guess so," I said as the full extent of what she was saying sank in.

"For goodness sake though didn't mention a word of this to my parents before they leave, mother would have a fit if she knew."

The car came early for Mum and Dad so we were left on our own to get ready for dinner. The girls took my bedroom as it was rather more organised than Barry's.

"Did Dominique explain that they are staying tonight?"

"Yer she said her father was more than pleased that he didn't have to check on her and that he is expecting us all to have lunch at the club tomorrow."

"Have you got any condoms?"

"No why should I?"

"Of course you should, here take two of mine, Dad gave them to me."

"Shit it must have been a serious sex talk."

"It was, believe me."

Marie excelled herself and prepared a dinner fit for a king. We started with vegetable soup, which she assured was had prepared from her own vegetable patch, followed by lobster salad. Her special pepper steak was to die for and rivalled anything served in the best London restaurant. The girls were very impressed.

"Your very lucky to have found such a good cook." Mandy commented as we finished.

"Well she came with the villa, we didn't exactly find her."

Barry glared at me and kicked me under the table and he accused me of being a snob.

"Shall we take coffee by the pool?" I said trying to deflect interest from the look of pain on my face.

"Yes that sounds perfect," Mandy said.

I went ahead and lit the garden touches. Profiteroles rolls and coffee was the perfect end to a spectacular meal and we sat watching the sun set across the hills.

"I wish I could live here all the time," said Mandy in a dream like voice.

"No. You would be bored inside a month."

"What are you meaning bored this is the most perfect place to be living."

"Oh I didn't mean it like that I just meant that Mandy would miss living in London." When would I learn to keep my big mouth shut.

"I suppose your right. It's just that every year I go away on holiday and end up wishing the same thing, that I didn't have to go home."

"Well we all go through the same thing, believe me I'm a doctor." There were giggles all round.

"So what now?" said Mandy looking around as if expecting to find something to do.

"Well we thought that some slow dancing would be in order since we had our fill of loud music last night."

"Sounds as if you are taking the piss of me again." We all laughed again.

"No of course not. Come on."

Barry and I had made a selection of romantic dance music earlier while the girls had finished changing for dinner. I just hate to leave everything till the last minute. Besides if they could plan to stay here without consulting us first we could at least choose a little slow dancing music.

We ended by dancing through a whole selection of Neil Diamond, Barry's choice not mine, taking time out for kissing breaks in between songs but towards the end I was beginning to get a bit tied of standing up, besides it was still very warm inside. Before I had time to suggest we take a break Mandy broke through my thoughts.

"I think its time for a swim. Last one in is a loser."

The dancing was over and we started running though the house towards the pool. We hadn't planned this. As I ran through the courtyard I nearly tripped on their dresses which had been discarded in great haste before they dived in. I reached the edge of the pool to find the other three already swimming about.

"Looks like your the loser Mr Wilde," said Mandy before diving under and sweeping Dominique off her feet.

Unfortunately Barry hadn't managed to get any of his cloths off before jumping in and was struggling to remove his shoes in the shallow end. The girls on the other hand seemed to have it down to a fine art and were now doing back stroke up the pool in their panties.

"Put the touches out before you get in and hurry up about it boy." Mandy yelled.

I did as I was told, slipped off my shirt and shorts and sat of the edge waiting for my body to familiarise itself with the temperature of the water.

"Come on get in and stop fucking about."

I hadn't heard Mandy use the F-word till now, too much wine at dinner no doubt. I slipped in and walked slowly towards the deep end, stopping briefly as the water came up to my balls. As I stood there contemplating my next move I was caught around the knees and dragged under. I came up coughing and spluttering.

"Oh did I scare you? Come here, poor baby." Mandy put her arms around me and kissed me.

After swimming about for a bit more we left Barry and Dominique in the pool and went into the house.

"I think we had better dry off before we both catch our death," I said.

I followed Mandy into my bedroom carefully studying the crack of her arse which was clearly visible as she walked.

"Here take this." She threw me a towel from the bathroom and then came back and began drying me off.

I took the towel she had given me and did the same. I gently dried her hair as she rubbed my chest and slowly dried my way down her body until I was crouching behind her and drying her legs. She moved her legs apart slightly to allow me to dry between them and I slowly made my way up towards her crotch. Just as I was about to get down to some serious drying she turned around.

"I think that's enough don't you?"

"Oh sorry I was just..."

"I know what you were just doing." She took the towel from me and threw both of them across the room and went over and turned the lights out.

"I think its time for bed don't you?" She took my hand in the dark and led me across the room. This is it I thought I am finally going to lose my virginity.

It never happened. We slept in the same bed and it never happened despite managing to talk her out of the rest of her underwear. I woke early again the next morning but instead of leaping out of bed I lay there, propped myself up on one arm and watched her sleep. She was so peaceful and so beautiful. She stirred a little while later and smiled as she looked across to find me watching her.

"Sleep well?" I asked.

"Yes thank you, it was a beautiful evening and you were the perfect gentleman."

Hmm I thought, there are no prizes for being the perfect gentleman in this life.

By the time Mum and Dad were dropped back the girls had long gone.

"Have a nice evening then?" Dad said as he walked in.

"Yes pretty quiet through."

Marie was magnificent and never breathed a word, the French have such a passion for romance. We met Dominique's father for lunch and despite one awkward moment when he very nearly let the cat out of the bag we had a very pleasant time.

"Some of my friends are having the beach party tonight would you like to come?"

"Yes that sounds great. What time?"

"Well it won't be starting until the sun goes down. Perhaps if it is all right with you Papa the boys could stay with us tonight."

I tried not to look surprised and instead glanced at my father.

"We have plenty of the room and its the least we could do."

"Fine I don't think that would be a problem, after last night we are both looking forward to some peace and quiet anyway."

"Its settled then." Dominique's father concluded.

I stopped Barry as we walked back to the car.

"What just happened then," I asked again.

"I have no idea but I think we're going to get lucky again tonight."

"What do you mean again? Your telling me you had sex last night?"

"And your telling me you didn't."

"Well Mandy is a nice girl."

"No fun to had going out with nice girls, plenty of time for that when you get married, its the bad ones you want to find. Dominique showed me positions last night I didn't even know existed, especially in the pool."

Bastard I thought to myself, I didn't really need to know that.

"Oh and you can have these back as well Dominique's on the pill."

What the hell was wrong with me? Why is it I always seemed to miss out? Bugger being the perfect gentleman. Besides why was it some guys have all the luck while others never seem to have any? Well one way or another I thought to myself, tonight's the night.

By the time we got there the beach party was in full swing and the girls ran to greet us as we walked down the beach. We were introduced around to Dominique's friends and I have to admit if Mandy had not been standing with me I wouldn't have known where to start. It must have something to do with the sun because this was the loveliest collection of creatures I had ever laid eyes on. We ran down the beach splashing water on each other, finally collapsing in each other arms some distance away.

"You know I really had a wonderful time last night it was perfect."

"Oh yer was it really?"

"Yes it was. I hope you weren't too disappointed nothing happened I didn't mean to be a tease."

"Well that's exactly what you are."

"Let's see what we can do to put things right then shall we?"

She rolled me on my back and climbed on top of me, easing the straps of her top off her shoulders. The moon shone through her hair as she lowered her head and began kissing me. I will never forget that night as long as I live. We made love for what seemed like hours, only returning to the fire as the embers began to die down. We walked back to the club just as the last punters were beginning to leave and made our way up stairs. Barry and Dominique were already asleep in the other bed so we undressed silently and slipped under the covers. We made love again one more time before falling asleep in each other arms. I woke as the sun began to rise and went over to shake Barry awake.

"I think we should get back to the spare bedroom."

"Do we have to?"

"Yes, otherwise Dominique's father is going to kill us." As he climbed out of bed the covers fell away.

"Just look at that would you."

We spent the rest of the week on and off the beach together but it passed too quickly. On the last night there was a fair in town so we had dinner and headed down there to see what was going on.

"We're leaving tomorrow," I said as we approached the fair ground.

"I know."

"I wish I could stay."

"I wish you could as well but it had to come to an end sometime. All holidays do. Besides I think you said that."

"I know I did. But it doesn't have to end we can still see each other when you get back to London."

"I don't think that's going to be possible."

"What do you mean don't you want to see me?"

"Yes of course I do its just that you live all the way up in Hertford and I live in London, it just wouldn't work, besides I start my A-Levels next year so I will be very busy."

My heart had begun to sink when the conversation started, by the time it finished it was in my stomach. We kissed for the last time as the Ferris wheel rose to its full height and then had to go as we had an early start the next morning. They waved to us as the car pulled away and we never saw either of them again. As I lay in bed that night I drew my long forgotten loneliness around me tightly and cried myself to sleep.

Samantha

I saw her upon nearer view,
A spirit, yet a woman too!
William Wordsworth

Back at school neither of us spoke much about what had had happened that summer, it was somehow too precious to be spoilt by close inspection and discussion.

Riding still featured largely in our lives. Dad had secured some managed stables for Allie and Ross and I took riding lessons there Saturday morning. Not that I really needed them but it gave me a legitimate excuse to hang around the stables and watch all those young girls go out riding in their jodhpurs.

That spring Allie become pregnant at last so I began to make a point of going up there most afternoons to check on her progress after school. Being pregnant seemed to suit her and her coat took on a glow I had never seen before.

"She looks brilliant doesn't she, it really seems to suit her." It was Sam, she was one of the stable hands. She always seemed to be there but I have to admit I had never really taken much notice of her, there were always too many other girls around on the weekend. She stood at the stable door with her chin resting on her hands folded carefully under each other. She carefully watching me as I deliberately brushed Allie's coat, she began to make me feel very uncomfortable. She let herself into the box.

"I didn't think you were usually here during the week."

"Mum had some calls to make so she dropped me off on her way though. It's certainly a surprise to see you here."

"Well I thought as Allie was pregnant I'd try and come up as much as possible just to be with her really until the foal is born."

"That's just be beautiful."

"Don't be so sarcastic."

"Who me?"

"Well are you just going to stand there or are you going to help me?"

"I can't I haven't changed."

"Oh poor baby."

"Well if your going to be like that." She turned and before I knew it she was gone.

I finished brushing Allie and came out of the box to look for her. I didn't have to look that far, she was sitting on the fence of the riding school smoking a cigarette.

"That will kill you know."

"Well I'd rather die young enjoying myself than conform to societys expectations."

"Oh big words for a little girl.

"Who are you calling a little girl?"

"You and what are you going to do about it?

"Beat your arse."

"Is that a promise of a threat Samantha?"

"A threat and don't call me Samantha." With that she threw away her butt, leapt of the fence and started running towards. I bent low and just as she reached me I span on my left foot. She kept going straight ahead and landed flat on her face in a pile of saw dust. She turned, her eyes flashing.

"Your going to have to do better than that. Can't stay I have homework. See you Samantha." I grabbed on my bike and headed for the lane.

No one can explain what is and isn't attractive about any one individual. Think about how many people you come into contact with throughout your life, only very few really make you stand up and pay attention. Of course as you go through your teenage age years with all those hormones running about in your veins you are somewhat less fussy. But even so every so often a special person comes alone and shakes the very foundations you live on. Susan was the first Sam was about to become the second.

I waited for her to turn up every afternoon as I brushed Allie but there was no sign of her. Saturday, I thought, she will definitely be there Saturday. I booked an extra lesson on Friday for Saturday afternoon. At least that would provide me with the appropriate excuse to spend the day there. Saturday finally arrived and I was up at the crack of dawn and arrived at the stables a full two hours before my lesson which was somewhat of a shock for the instructor.

"What are you doing here so early the lesson isn't for another two hours yet."

"Well I thought I'd spend some time with Allie," I replied rather sheepishly.

I wandered off to find Allie and as I walked the field I stopped short and said out loud: "What the hell have you got to feel guilty about? You haven't done anything wrong all you did was turn up early."

Allie was off feeding on some long grass which was still covered with dew from the night before. She raised her head momentarily as I approached and then went back to eating. I stood beside her and put her arms round her neck.

"How can someone effect you so much when you've only spoken to them once?" I asked half expecting her to answer. "I don't even know anything about her except her names Sam. Samantha Wilde. Stop it." I led Allie back to the stables.

The lesson went without event, not that I was paying much attention, I was watching out for Sam. She was no where to be seen. I stayed for the second lesson. No Sam. I brushed Allie again and left. As I cycled home in the growing darkness I chastised myself for being so stupid. What do you think your doing. She hates you. Any wonder she hasn't been to the stables since you humiliated her in that pile of saw dust. Besides she's not your type. I tried to put her out of my mind. I didn't go to see Allie that next week it seemed there was always too much to do after school. I was late as usual for my lesson the next Saturday and mother conceded to drive me. As we pulled into the courtyard I spotted Sam sitting on the fence. My heart leap into my mouth.

"Your late," she said as I passed her.

"I know," I said dismissively not looking up.

"Toni's been waiting."

"All right for Christ's sake."

Women. I rode very badly that morning, unable to make Star do anything I wanted. Sam sat and watched. They say horses react badly to girls having their period. Sam must be having hers. I walked out through the gate when it was over towards the stables.

"You rode like shit this morning.

"No thanks to you rag girl."

"What's that supposed to mean?"

"You heard."

She jumped off the fence and followed me over to the tack room.

"Look I'm sorry I didn't mean to embarrass you."

"Yer well you shouldn't have sat there watching."

"I was having a break, I was here at the crack of dawn this morning trying to catch up. Besides you usually ride so gracefully."

I turned to look at her. She put on her best 'little girl lost look,' my anger subsided, she really was trying to apologise. But for what, not turning up last week or putting me off this morning. I looked at her trying to determine which, I couldn't.

"Have I done something to upset you?"

"What you mean apart from being an annoying little madam?" This time she really did look hurt. "What happened to you last weekend anyway?" Her face brightened immediately.

"I had a piano recital in London on Saturday, we spent the day down there."

"You play the piano?"

"Yes I play the piano and I'm good, no need to sound so surprised."

"I'm not, well maybe a little..." Time to change the subject. "Come and help me brush Allie I haven't been here all week."

"I know." We brushed her in silence, both immersed in our private thoughts.

Our friendship grew along with the foal inside Allie.

One afternoon we were sitting outside the stables taking a break both of us looking out over the fields not really talking when she mumbled something under her breath.

"What?"

"I said are you coming to the spring dance, are you deaf or something?"

"No I'm not. What dance?"

"The dance this Saturday night."

"I didn't know there was one."

"Well now you do are you coming?"

"I don't know I'll have to go home and check my diary." Perhaps I shouldn't have said that.

"You keep a diary?"

"Yes otherwise I'd never know what I was doing," I said rather defencively. "Nothing wrong with boys keeping a diary."

"I bet its just full of girls phone numbers and nothing else."

"That goes to show how much you know."

Actually I did know about the spring dance, I'd known for weeks and had been trying to figure out who to ask to find out if she was going.

"I'll let you know tomorrow, I need to get home I have a physics assignment which has to be in tomorrow."

"Sorry to disturb you professor, I guess I'll see you tomorrow then."

"Yes I guess." I really did have a physics assignment to get on with but it didn't have to be handed in until Friday, I just needed time to think.

We met up again at the stables the next afternoon. "I have re-arranged my schedule and it looks like I'll be able to make in Saturday night. How about I meet you here, we can walk out to the woods together."

"Fine." I took this as a yes and buried myself in my school work until Saturday. I always imagined that as you got older the whole dating and mating game would get easier. It never does in fact if anything it gets harder. The more rejections you get the less likely you are to ask someone out on a date and if you do it only takes the slightest rejection to put you off.

As I approached the stables I could see the fire at the edge of the woods, sending slow burning sparks high into the air. Sam was leaning against the gate post, the small ember of her cigarette just visible in her hand.

"You made it then."

"Of course. Are you ready?"

"No I'm just standing here about to bag up that pile of shit over there."

"All right, all right. I guess I should have arranged to pick you up."

"That would of been nice but I don't think my mother would have been to impressed."

"Why not? She thinks I'm staying at a friends house tonight."

"And are you?"

"Yes and this is just a photographic reproduction you see before you."

"I think you need a drink."

"I know I do."

The dance was a blast, it was put on each year by the owner of the stables for all the workers and the people who boarded their horses at the stables. By the time the fire was beginning to die down we were both pretty drunk and started back off in the direction of the stables. After much stumbling and falling we finally made it. Sam produced a key from around her neck and unlocked the tack room door."

"Come on I have a bottle hidden here somewhere."

She switched on the light, pushed me inside and pulled the door closed behind her.

"Now where did I put that bottle? Ah here it is and produced a bottle of cider from under one of the saddles."

"What exactly have you been planning then?"

"Well I wasn't sure if you were going to turn up or not tonight so I liberated this from my older sisters bedroom knowing that if you didn't make it I won't be going to the dance alone so at least I could get drunk."

"She unscrewed the cap and took a mouthful, now that better, here," and handed me the bottle. "Ever noticed how wonderful leather smells?"

"What do you mean?"

"You know rich and sexy."

"I've never really thought about it before." I sat down against the far wall, my head resting in the bridles hanging above. "Come here and sit down you look like your waiting for a bus."

"I may as well of been its been so slow coming."

She walked over, stood at my feet, the electricity sparking between us. Slowly she crouched down and then simply fell into my body, our lips met and we began kissing wildly as the lust that had been building between us was finally unleashed. I reached round behind her and grabbed at her cheeks, digging my fingers into her flesh. My hands found the crack of her arse and I followed it down between her legs, she moaned as my fingers reached her crotch and her growing wetness. Eventually we broke apart desperate for air and another drink.

"So where did you learn to kissed like that? I asked as she necked the bottle again.

"Wouldn't you like to know."

"Actually, yes I would."

She looked at me for a long time. "Better than telling you I'll show you, here give me your hand."

Before I knew what she was doing she took my right wrist and looped it through one of the bridles.

"What do you think you doing?"

"Just relax and give me you other hand." She took it and did the same on the other side."

"There, comfortable? Now stand up and turn around."

"Why? Just do as your told." I struggled to stand, finally gaining my feet.

"Now turn around and bend over." I turned around watching her over my left shoulder as she took a small riding crop from the shelf."

"What are you going to do with that?

"I told you I was going to whip your arse, this is landing me in the saw dust that day."

She raised the crop slightly and bought it down across my cheeks. "That hurt."

"Don't be such a baby," and bought the crop down harder this time. Shit, I studied the the old timber which made up the wall in front of me. And again.

"When I get out of here I'm going to whip your arse good and proper."

"Big words for a little boy" She bought the crop down again.

I hadn't noticed it immediately but my dick was at full attention. Enough was enough. I struggled to get my hands loose, finally pulling the bridles off their nails. I shook my hands loose. She was going to get it now. I caught her round the waist just as she was heading out the door, lifting her off her feet and deposited her over a saddle on one of the wooden horses. I snatched the crop from the floor where it had fallen flung her dress up over her head and pulled her panties down. I raised the crop and bought it down across her naked buttocks, she squired on the horse but didn't attempt to get off. Taking it a little higher each time I gave her six quick lashes in succession. She was enjoying this. Personally I had the biggest hardon I could remember and it was busting to get out of my jeans. I threw the crop down and grabbed her cheeks hard, alternatively rubbing the red marks which were beginning to appear and digging my fingers into her tight bum. I spread her legs apart and stared at her dripping gash. I teased her for a minute or two but she was having now of it.

"Stop pissing about, stick your fingers up me, fuck me with your fingers and slap my arse."

Two fingers slipped in easily and she began to rock back and forth on them, literally fucking my hand, she came within seconds.

"Now get that dick out of yours and fuck me good and hard."

I didn't need to be asked twice. I removed my fingers, wiped them on her ass, fumbled with my jeans and slipped my dick home. Boy that felt good. As the pace picked up I bought my hand down and slapped her on each cheek in turn.

"Harder, fuck my harder! Yes you dirty bastard!"

I couldn't last much longer and we both came with a yell I thought would surely bring the neighbours running. We stayed like that for a few moments as we regained our breath and eventually I pulled her up and we fell into each others arms in a heap on the floor.

"Where did you learn to do that, you don't seem the type," she asked.

"I had an excellent foreign teacher," I said watching her closely as see shifted to lie on her side.

"Does that hurt, I didn't mean to hurt you."

"You didn't I'm fine. That was the best sex I've had in a long time."

"Where did all that come from then the riding crop and all I mean?"

"Ah well that's a secret from my past."

"Well go on then tell me."

"I don't think I should it might get you over excited again."

"That's a risk you'll have to take. Besides if you don't I'll have to give you a few more stokes. Now are you going to tell me?"

"Is that a promise or a threat?"

I grabbed the crop from where it had fallen, rolled her over and pretented I was going to whip her again.

"Alright, alright, you win, I'll tell." I loosened my grip and she crawled up and lay her head on my chest and began her story.

"When I was young there was a group of us who used to play together up in the woods where we were tonight. Cowboys and Indians was our favourite game and it inevitably ended up with the older boys forcing us girls to stand facing a tree, then they would pull our dresses up and gently whip us with small branches."

She raised her head to look at me and guage my reaction and then laid her head down and continued.

"As you can imagine this eventually turned into a real game of wills, I don't think the cowboy and indian bit came in to it much after a while. They would chase us all over, eventually catching us then we would refuse to turn around pretending not to want our bums beaten. After much twoing and frowing they would each grab one of us, pin us down on the ground, spin us over, half sit on our backs, feel us up for a while and then slap our bare arses at the same time. Here I think you had better bring me off again while I finish, this story never fails to get me horny." She moved slightly so I could reach between her legs.

"Us girls used to talk about it as we walked home, each assuring the other it wasn't going to happen tomorrow, each secretly wishing tomorrow was here already so we could do it again. Every day for about two months I walked home with wet panties, falling asleep each night playing with myself thinking about the previous afternooons events. Then one afternoon my mother came looking for me as one of the horses had escaped and dicovered Rick sitting on me, my panties round my ankles and his fingers doing their best to bring me off, which he had done regularly I might add." She rubbed herself harder against my hand as she finished this part.

"Mum went spare, forbidding me ever to go up there again. Well all those memories came flooding back tonight as we sat round the fire. I decided that if I could just get you back here afterwards there was a pretty good chance I could get you to whip me."

"Oh you did did you?"

"Yes and I was right!"

We never did repeat that particular senerio but I can remember it as if it was yesterday.

Barry continued to be a constant source of amusement. Since his mother worked such long hours they had a women come in to clean once a week just to keep the house in order. She was actually an old friend of Mrs Russell's and quite a character and we often went round there for a chat on Thursday afternoons. By the time we got there she would be sitting in the kitchen catching up on the soaps in her break. She'd make us tea and always had some freshly baked cake sitting ready to slice. She had a fourteen year old daughter Susan who went to the local school and when Susan finished she would come by to help her mother finish off and get a lift home. Barry had fancied her for as long as I can remember and had gone to extrodinary lengths to attact her attention. He used to make a habit of taking a shower when he got home from school so that by the time Susan was ready to clean the bathroom she would always manage to walk in on him standing in the middle of the floor, completely naked, apologising for having left the door unlocked and promising to remember to lock it next week. Of course she knew exactly what was going on and never failed to disturb him in the bathroom each week. But that's as far as it ever went. You have to hand it to him though his persistence eventually paid off because on her fifteenth birthday he finally persuaded her into his bed. Unfortunately for him it came to an abrupt end about three weeks later when her mother arrived home early to find Susan in bed which she immediately interrupted as being strange and on opening the wardrobe door found Barry standing in amongst her clothes just wearing a pair of jockey shorts. For once his luck had deserted him.

"Right then we're off see you, "Dad said as they headed out the door, "we should be home around midnight."

They were going on an office night out to the threatre which he arranged occasionally as a treat for the office staff. Although I enjoyed living at home that particular night I was looking forward to some peace and quiet since I desperately needed to catch up with my English which I'd let slip with all that had gone on in the last month or so. I was sitting there reading when the phone rang. I'm not going to answer it I thought, I'll just let the machine take it. Five rings and sure enough the message began.

...please leave your message after the tone...Beep.

"Pick up the phone for Christ's sake it's time," I heard Sam yell into the phone, "come on I know your there."

I relented. "Hi, I didn't hear the phone ring, sorry."

"Forget all that now you have to get down here."

"What for I have work to do for next week, besides I saw you this morning."

"Screw that Allie's having the foal, you have five minutes to get here or I'm going to kill you," and she slammed the phone down.

Shit this is all I needed tonight, why is it than when you really need them parents are never around. I grabbed my bike from the garage and raced down to the stables in the dark. By the time I arrived Allie's water had broken and she was rapidly nearing the time of delivery.

"What do you want me to do?"

"Go to the tack room, grab some of the clean rags in the sack by the window, bring them back here and then go an put the kettle on."

I did as I was told and arrived back at the stable just as she was giving birth. It was amazing to watch and sent shivers down my spine, a new life was beginning with a host of possibilities before it. We'd discussed the matter at home before and decided that we would keep the foal at least for the first twelve months with a view to selling it at the yearling sales next year.

"It a boy, a beautiful red coated boy, he's perfect."

The foal lay down where he'd been borne as his mother attended to the afterbirth and when she'd finished he began the stuggle to find his feet. After several tries he eventually gained his feet and stumbled around the stable as he learnt to deal with the force of gravity.

After making sure he was feeding we headed for the kitchen and coffee.

"I'm just glad you were here and rang me, Dad is going to be gutted he missed it."

She smiled. I couldn't be sure but I don't think they really saw eye to eye about the horses. Whether it had anything to do with the horses though I'm not sure either, I don't think he really approved of us hanging around together, although he was yet to say anything to me, there was just an unspoken tension between them.

"It was beautiful wasn't it?"

"Yer you never get used to the shear enormity of the act."

"Have you ever thought of having any?" she asked.

"No I think people would stare if I took a foal out to the park in its pram."

"Not a foal you idiot, childen!"

"Oh, well yes, I think I would like to have two, one of each."

"What about you then?" I watched while the expression changed on her face to one of serious contemplation.

"No, too much responsibility, besides I don't know whether I even want to get married yet."

"Well you'll begin to feel different when your biological clock begins ticking. And another thing if you leave it too late the children will turn out to be mentally retarded."

"Who told you that then?"

"No one it's a medical fact." Actually I wasn't sure it was a medical fact, Barry told me as much once when we were discussing Mrs Spence being pregent. She lived a few doors up from Barry and had to be about 37 when she announced she was pregenent. Mother thought it was a disgrace, a women of her age having a baby. They'll be retired before he finishes university she said when I told her. Despite being wonderfully modern about most things occasionally she would forget what she was saying imagining as I did repeating something her mother would have said. We checked on the foal once more and I went home to finish off my reading. I was right, Dad was gutted.

We continued to see each other all that year, keeping a close eye on the foal and his progress. He was eventually named Tacks which, although my parents didn't understand why, was of course a reference to that first night together in the Tack Room. It was our secret and bought on gails of laughter when ever we talked about it and knowing glances exchanged when anyone else was around. Being able to share such a secret only increased the bond between us. In ways which are difficult to explain though she was also dangerous This danger tended to surface in her very strong sexual nature. I often wondered what would happen if this was ever given its full leash.

As often as possible Saturday afternoons were spent riding the bridleways which fanned out from the stables. More often than not these rides ended up with us making love in some very unusal places. One particular afternoon we left the horses to graze under some trees and walked down towards a corn field owned by one of the local farmers.

"I'll race you to the scarecrow," said Sam as we neared the edge of the field and took off like a scared rabbit.

The corn must have been almost ready to harvest because apart from the movement of the storks she was completely lost from sight. I went after her heading in the general direction of the scarecrow in the middle of the field but not really knowing where I was going. Running flat out, pushing the corn from my path, I suddenly stumbled into a small clearing and the scarecrow. I pulled up short and Sam jumped out from behind it, stark naked, and shouted 'Boo' at the top of her voice nearly scaring me half to death. I lunghed for her knocking her to the ground. We wrestled playfully throwing each other over and over until she ended up sitting on my chest, pinning my arms behind my head.

"Now I'm going to have my wicked way with you," she said.

She proceeded to do just that as the heavens opened up and a late summer rain storm broke over us. As she continued the rain poured down on us both, two particular tracks deciding to leave her body via the ends of her nipples. We laughed uncontrollable and eventually fell into each others arms when we finished, laying back we drank rain from the sky as lightening flashed all around us and huge black thunder clouds rolled by overhead. I remember lying there wondering if life could get any better than this. The horses looked up at us as we came back to them almost as if to say what the hell have you two been doing? We were covered from head to toe in mud and had to hose each other down when we got back to the stables.

With all that took place that year the following spring seemed to come round ever so quickly. When I was young, especially before we moved, the weeks seemed to roll by very slowly especially those long summer holidays which went on for ever and Christmas was always a very long time away. But a year had passed and it was time to take Tacks to the yearling sales in London. I was up early that morning to prepare the horse box and brush him down before we took off. Sam was already there when I arrived looking very tired and somewhat upset.

"Have you been crying?" I asked her carefully.

"No of course not what makes you think that?"

"Your eyes are all red."

"Well I didn't sleep much last night if you must know."

"Alright I was just asking." I began to brush Tacks watching her wander around attending to this and that as she went. Just as I was finishing his mane she came up behind me and put her arms around my waist and rested her head between my shoulders.

"He's leaving today," she said softly. I stopped brushing and turned round so her head lay on my chest.

"I know."

"He's so beautiful and I'll never see him again."

"I know but Dad said we could only keep him for the first year even before he was born."

"It's still not fair, he was our horse and now your fathers selling him just to make some money."

"Now come on that's not exactly fair, we've all become very attached to him especially me but you know how much work it would be to train him properly this year and I have to concertrate on my A-Levels, I just don't have the time, as much as I would like to."

"I know, I know it just feels like a part of us is being taken away and things will never be the same."

I held her for a while longer but we really had to get going. Her eyes were filled with tears and I wiped them away with the corner of my shirt.

"Come on Dad will be here any minute and if we are not ready to go he won't be best pleased."

"Yer well tough."

We finished loading Tacks into the trailer just as Dad pull up in the yard."

"Ready?"

"Yes all done," I replied.

"Right then hook that trailer up and lets hit the road."

The sale was extremely exciting and Tacks fetched a good price eventually going to an Irish trainer. He was due to leave at the end of the week. I had virtually forgotten the conversation we had had that morning until the ride home, hardly a word was spoken. Sam could not have been more acurate with what she had said earlier that day. It was as if something left us that day and we never quite recovered. As the weeks went on we spoke less and less until eventually she stopped coming to the stables Saturday's. I tried to ring her a few times but she always seemed to be out and I eventually let it drop and stopped calling. She was truly special.

Peta

I pray that he will see me
As I think I am.
Richard Overcombe.

Two months before my final A-Level exams my teeth began to turn from a slight annouance into a real problem. I had had a nagging ache in the back of my head for some time now and knew exactly what it was, my wisdom teeth were coming up, it had been a topic of conversation last time I was at the dentist. However the ache had started to get so bad I was finding it almost impossible to concentrate on my studies. Mother finally got fed up with my constant whinging and despite my protests dragged me off to the dentist.

We had been going there for years yet I still felt extremely uneasy sitting in that sterile waiting room, despite the abundance of lovely young nurses in short uniforms rushing with hushed foot steps between examination rooms.

"Charles, Charles Wilde?"

"Yes?"

"Doctor will see you next."

A delightful young nurse stood in the doorway of the waiting room smiling broadly at me. She spoke with a thick South African accent and seemed to be undressing me with her eyes. I shook my head don't be stupid its all in your imagination.

Mother tapped me on the arm. "Are you alright."

"Oh yes as right as right can be thank you."

I stood up and followed her through the surgery. I was right first time it was all my imagination.

She asked me to take a seat and left the room saying: "doctor will be with you shortly."

Sure enough Doctor Short walked in not a moment later, his teeth gleaming as he smiled as if to say look how good it can get.

"Well Charles we haven't seen you for a while. What's been happening then?" he asked as he motioned for me to open my mouth and began to poke around in there with some tools which looked like they had been cast in hell.

"Nothin mucth, I justh seem to haveth this pain in the bacth of my headth."

"Hmm well we'll see what we can do shall we?"

The nurse came back into the room and looked on dispassionately over his shoulder. I got a disturbing feeling she was enjoying this. He poked about for a little while longer and then glanced at the nurse and announced it was time for X-Rays. Now I have never been one to question the wisdom of medical science but ever since I found out X-rays could effect your sex life I had become extremely wary of such suggestions.

"Is that absolutley necessary," I said in my very best little boy lost voice.

"It's definitely your wisdom teeth that are giving you all the trouble as we discussed last time you were here but I really need to take some X-Ray's to determine just where we're at."

"Don't worry," Doctor Short said, "it won't effect your manhood." He had read my mind.

"Fine then just get on with it."

It turned out the wisdom teeth coming up on both sides of my mouth were beginning to put pressure on my back teeth which was causing all the discomfort. He called mother in and between them they agreed I should be scheduled to go into hospital next week to have them all out at once, this was not good chama.

Barry looked on in glee as I explained I was going into hospital next week to have my wisdom teeth out.

"Your face blows up like a balloon you know and won't come down for weeks."

This was all I needed, encouragement and support from the habinger of doom.

Sure enough my appointment was confirmed the next day and I was scheduled to go into hospital Sunday night. This was definitely not good chama. The hospital was a newly built complex out in the middle of no where and as we drove up the long drive to reception the feeling of doom began to grow. I didn't want my face to blow up like a balloon and stay that way for weeks, more importantly I didn't want to have any needles, I hated needles, in fact I hated the thought of needles. Why couldn't they just give me something to dull the pain and let me go home now? It was too late we were through the enterance and waiting in reception. Maybe I could slip out later and no one would ever notice, you know how disorganised hospitals are. Not this one. A nurse came up and stood before us in a chrisp white uniform.

"You must be Mr Wilde. I see you have your bags with you, although you won't be needing much, we prefer to dress lightly around here."

I see, a sense of humour into the bargin.

"There's no need for your parents to come with you now. Mr and Mrs Wilde we shall see you tomorrow evening, visiting hours are between 8 pm and 10 pm."

"Right then Mr Wilde follow me." And with that she turned on her heel and headed for the elevator.

"Well I guess I'll see you tomorrow then minus a few body parts, just hope they have it clear which bits they are taking out."

More humor. I grabbed my bags and began to walk slowly in the direction of where the nurse stood holding the elevator door open.

"Come along Mr Wilde its time you were settled in before lights out."

It turned out I had a private room overlooking the black countryside, comforting. I suppose it could have been worse, I could be dead, then again if it all went horribly wrong tomorrow I could be. I stoppped that train of thought there and then. As I unpacked my things the nurse bought in a gown for me to put on and a sign to go above my bed.

NILL BY MOUTH.

She took the water from beside my bed. "Now Mr Wilde do you know what this means?"

"I'm not allowed to eat anything?"

"Very good but it also means you are not allowed to drink anything. I have activated the nill by mouth button for your room which means the water is turned off in the bathroom so don't go ringing your buzzer when you find the taps don't work. Of course we do trust you, it's really just a precaution, should remove the temptation for you to take a midnight sip. Lights go out in an hour and there will be two flashes a minute before they do. You're free to wander around the ward but don't disturb any of the other patients. And remember nill by mouth means just that. The buzzer is on the panel beside the bed if you need anything. Now I'll say goodnight."

"Yes good night." She closed the door on her way out and left me to finish unpacking. I undressed and put the gown on she'd left me. Mind you it could hardly be called a gown as the entire back of it sprang open to the atmosphere as soon as you did anything apart from stand deadly still. (Bad choice of words).

Holding the night gown closed behind my back I decided that a quick tour of the ward was in order before turning in for the night. I went left out in the corridor, electing to walk in the opposite direct from the nurses station, and began my inspection. Doors led off into other private rooms from either side. The majority were closed but occassionally I came across an open one and glanced in as I walked by. Reaching the end of the corridor I found the recreation room and stuck my head in. The television was on but nobody was there. I decided this was a waste of time and started back to my room. I passed three more closed doors but then as I approached the fourth I could hear the sounds of a television. I slowed down and looked in.

"Hi." I jumped.

"Sorry I didn't mean to frighten you

"You didn't, I mean I shouldn't be disturbing you."

"Your not, I'm bored out of my head come in. My names Peta.

"Hi, I'm Charles."

"Nice to meet you Charles." Laying on the bed propped up with what looked like a dozen pillows was a young girl about fourteen or fifteen. Her face seemed to shine under the harsh hospital lights despite the fact that it was slightly shaded by a baseball cap.

"I see you haven't quite gotten used to hospital attire," she said motioning to my hand still holding the back of the night gown closed.

I let it go. "No I haven't, not really."

"Are you wearing anything under it?"

"Of course I am."

"Well what are you worrying about, I don't bother anymore, if someone sees the lot then good luck to them, nothing to see anyway."

"So what are you in for?" she asked raising herself of the pilllows slightly.

"I'm having my wisdom teeth out tomorrow morning so don't offer me anything to eat or drink I'm not allowed."

"Oh you poor thing, I guess I'm just going to have to eat all these chocolates by myself then." she proceeded to unwrap two and slowly put them in her mouth, all the time watching for a reaction from me.

"I think I had better go, I don't know how strong my will power to resist is and I'd rather not find out." I got up to leave and the smile left her face almost immediately.

"I'm sorry that was cruel, I'll put them away, don't go you're the only person I've seen all day except the nurses and their as boring as petrified piles of dinasour shit."

I sensed an almost desperate tone in her voice and, seeing that she generally looked sorry, I sat down again.

"So what are you in for then?" I began.

"Oh I've been in and out of here since I was born and they still don't know what's wrong with me. No doubt it has something to do with my mental parents."

"Your parents are physcos?"

"No no not like that they're are just weirder than the average parents."

"Oh I see," but I didn't really.

"Want to see a photo of them, you can see it in their eyes."

She leaned over to get the picture from her far bedside table, her gown falling away for a moment. She was telling the truth she really didn't bother wearing anything else. Turning back to me she fixed me with a grin.

"Now wasn't that worth hanging around for? The male trainee nurses seem to enjoy that particular move the most."

She handed me a picture of her family sitting under a huge oak tree at what looked like a picnic. She sat in between what I assumed were her two sisters, again wearing the baseball cap.

"Are these you sisters then?

"Yes, the one on the left is Nancy and on the right is Drew."

"Nancy and Drew sounds like the childrens author."

"Very good, you see not only are my parents weird my father is a writer with a sick sense of humour, hence the names."

"So what happened to you then?"

"Before I was born my mother went to a fortune teller to find out whether she was having a boy or a girl. The fortune teller told her there was no doubting it she was carrying a boy so they picked the name Peter, you know as in Peter Pan. Of course when I came out and they discovered I was a girl the idea of changing my name seemed too much like hard work so they just adjusted the ending and hence Peta."

Just then the lights went out once, then twice.

"I think I had better be getting back, it must be time for lights out."

"Oh don't worry about that there is plenty of time.

"So where do you live then?"

"Hertford, it's not all that far from here."

"Yes I know my parents have a property just outside Hunnsden."

"Really! Hunnsden is a lovely little village we often go there for lunch on a Sunday during the winter, I'm surprised I haven't seen you round before."

"Oh we don't get out much, the farm keeps us pretty busy all year round." Just then the lights went out.

"I think its time I was going, I just hope I can find my way back in the dark."

"Don't worry what room number are you?"

"336 I think."

"If you go straight out my door, across the corridor and feel your way along the wall to the first door you are just four doors up from that."

"You certainly know your way around here."

"Well I aught to." I got up from my chair and just as I was about to turn to where I thought the door was I felt Peta's hand grab my arm.

"Don't I get a good night kiss?"

I moved over to the edge of the bed meaning to kiss her on the cheek but instead my lips came directly in contact with hers and as they made contact she opened her mouth slightly and slipped her tongh into my mouth. Not really knowing what to do I responded by doing the same, each of us exploring the others mouths. What she lacked in technique she certainly made up for with enthusiasm. Finally I broke away not wishing for her to discover the hard on which was developing under my night gown. I made my apologies and felt my way to the door.

"Thank you Charles for my first real kiss." I looked back into the room and tried to see the outline of her lying on the bed but couldn't.

"Good night Peta."

Despite my circumstances I slept well that night dreaming about a girl wearing a big straw hat with golden hair streaming out behind her as she ran. As we rolled over and over down a hill of long green grass the end of my dream was cut short. I became aware that the pain in my arm was not from rolling down the hill but from the nurse shaking me awake.

"You were certainly off in another world just now."

"Yer and it was much more pleasant that being here," I snapped back.

"So who got out of the wrong side of the bed then."

"You by look of your make up."

"Now Mr Wilde no need to get personal."

"Fine then just leave me alone and let me sleep."

"I'm afraid that's impossible the anaesthesiologist will be here any moment to give you your injection."

"My injection?"

"I'm sure the surgeon will explain it all Mr Wilde, in the mean time just make yourself comfortable and they'll be alone shortly."

I tried to concentrate my mind on other things such as watching Peta roll over in bed last night but it was no good the thought of that huge needle was too much. I waited.

Hours seemed to pass, well actually about ten minutes, before there was a knock on the door and in walked two impossibly tall men dressed in blue, one holding a silver tray, the contents of which I couldn't quite see.

"Good morning Mr Wilde and how are you this fine morning?

"I've been better."

"Well I'm sure things are going to improve once we have those nasty wisdom teeth of yours in a jar what?"

"I'm Dr Gutling and this is Mr Simon's. He is going to give you your injection and then in about an hour the nurse will be back to take you up to threate. From there on in its all down hill . The next thing you know you will be waking up, it will all be over and it will be time to go home."

Mr Simon's stepped up to the bed when Dr Gutling had finished, placed the tray on the bedside table and start fiddling about with a packet trying to open it. I desperately tried not to look into the tray but just could help myself. Sure enough sitting in the tray was a syringe end and what looked like huge needle cover by a plastic sleave. He finally got the packet open, picked up the syringe, pulled off the end and started to draw the anaesthetic out of the vile. I couldn't look any longer and had to turn my head away.

"That's it Mr Wilde, turn over, time for your injection."

From the tone in his voice it sounded as if he was announcing it was time to play musical chairs at a childrens birthday party. I bet his mother used to give him enemas when he was young. He lifted up my gown saying it wouldn't hurt a bit and proceeded to stick me with his huge needle. I bit down on my tounge saving my cry until they had left the room and were no longer looking at my arse. Shit that hurt. I lay back as comfortably as is possible considering I had just been fately wounded and waited for the anaesthetic to take effect. It didn't take long. I lay there drifting in and out of sleep trying to recapture the dream I had been disturbed from this morning when once again I felt this pulling on my arm. It was the bloody nurse.

"Time to head up to threate Mr Wilde, now slide over on to the trolley, that's it."

I was wheeled up to the threatre and left in the hallway outside. Everyone that passed seemed to be looking straight up my gown. I lay there watching the ceiling tiles move ever so slightly, they thought I couldn't see them but you could if you watched really closely. The nurse came back, lent right over until she was about two inches from my face and said it time to go. We went through two huge plastc doors, which nearly took one of my arms clear off at the shoulder, the journey ending with me studying the enormous eyebrow which Dr Gutling must have grown since this morning.

"The nurse is going to place this mask over your nose and mouth, I want you to breath normally and count backwards from ten."

"Ten, nine, eight sev..."

Something has just shit in my mouth and then covered it up with dirt, this was the first thought I had as I began to come round later that afternoon. I lay there for a while trying to unstick my tounge from the roof of my mouth before slowly opening my eyes. It was very dark in the room except for a thin sliver of light all around the curtains on the window. Either I've died and this is hell and they haven't lit the evening fires or the curtains are closed and it is still daylight outside. I opted for hell and decided to see if my nurse buzzer would bring me a naked nurse with horns. The buzzer didn't seem to work I tried it again. Nothing. Again. This time the door opened and in walked my naked nurse. No, unfortunately this was not hell and this was not my naked nurse.

"I see your back in the land of the living." I tried to ask for water but it was no good I couldn't speak.

"Now don't try and speak instead I want you to listern. Don't try and get up and for goodnes sake don't attempt to drink anything. I know your mouth is uncomfortable right now but unless you want to be ill you must do as I say. I'll come and see you a little while later and bring you a mouth bath."

A mouth bath want the hell was that when it was at home. She left the room. All I could think about as I lay there was how wonderful a big glass of mountain spring water would be and what a relief it would be to get this discusting taste out of my mouth. I lay there a little while longer and then decided to make a break for the bathroom, maybe they had turned the taps back on again. Eventually finding the light switch, I waited for my eyes to adjust and then eased my arms back and slowly raised myself up on my elbows, this was going to be easy. I bought my knees up to my chest and then swung my legs down over the edge of the bed. I bought myself upright, all the time watching the door, half expecting the nurse to come back any moment. I put my feet on the floor, stood up and nearly passed out. Luckily I had a tight hold on the bed and managed to stay up right. Somehow, although I don't really rememeber much, I managed to make it to the bathroom and found myself starring at the taps in front of me. I managed to avoid looking at myself in the mirror. Please have turned the water on, I'm going to die of dehydration. I turned on cold tap and out ran the water into the basin. I put my hand under the running water and bought some up to my lips. Necture of the gods. I carefully swallowed a little and feeling two hundred percent better headed back to bed and fell immediately asleep.

Some time later the nurse came back and gave me my mouth bath. She raised me up a little saying that my visitors would be in soon. Great, just what I feel like visitors, its a good thing I had time for my mouth bath before they arrived. I dozed some more only to be distrubed by the nurse saying its virgin time or was it visitors time. I opened my eyes and saw mother, father and Barry each standing by a face of the bed, dad right at the end, she must have said visitor. This was a real treat, I didn't think dad would make it, he hated hospitals, couldn't stand the smell of the places, makes me feel all weak at the knees he used to say. Yet there his was standing at the end of the bed to support his son in his hour of need. Mother started talking about something or other, none of which I really remember, I was too busy concentrating on the growing feeling that I wanted to be violently ill. Still unable to speak all of a sudden sat bolt upright in bed and projectile vomited a river of blood down the bed.

I was too busy turning my insides to outsides to remember what happened next but evidently this was too much for my father who immediately fainted, hitting his head on the radiator on the way down. (His favorite all time story is telling of how he woke up surrounded by nurses fussing over him. He thought he had died and gone to heaven. Barry went rushing out of the room never to darken the side of my bed again.

I woke the next morning and was allowed a small amount to drink and by the afternoon was feeling much better. After jelly for dinner I decided it was time to go for a walk and to see what Peta was doing. Taking very small steps and gripping the rail which ran the length of the corridor, I made my way down to her room, she wasn't there. Not thinking too much about it I went back to bed and promptly fell fast asleep. The next day I was to be discharged and mother came to pick me up.

"We felt it best after last time that your father should stay home. Your face doesn't look too bad now does it?"

Actually my face had blown up to twice its normal size, I stood looking at myself in the mirror that morning thinking it was probably a good thing Peta was not in her room, no doubt I would have scared her half to death. As we passed the nurses station I stopped to say thank you.

"By the way say hi to Peta for me would you?" The nurses both looked at each.

"What, what is it?"

"I'm sorry we thought you knew, Peta passed away the night before last."

Lolly

There are perfumes on my body and fresh leaves
upon my hair...

Francis Saltus

Right up until I sat down for the last time and opened the final paper I felt sure there was no way I was going to pass my A-Levels. However, when it was all over, I felt reasonably confident that I would get the marks I needed to be accepted into Cambridge. It had been a long hard struggle after the operation and all that business to do with Peta. Somehow though I had managed to focus my mind on the job at hand long enough to do about the right amount of work and was pleasantly surprised at how they had all fell out in the end. Desperately in need of a break I began to arrange to take a vacation travelling on The Continent for a couple of months. Barry was all for it and although limited by funds agreed to join me in the end. Rome was as good a place to start as any and besides Italy had been number two behind France on the list last year and look how well that turned out. Mother booked our tickets to Rome, organised the student rail passes and also booked open return tickets Paris-London. At least if we ran out of money we could still get home, drying from starvation perhaps but home. The plan was to fly into Rome, spend a couple of days there, catch a train down to the Italian riviera. Stay there for about four weeks. Travel up to Munich by train for the beer feast then on to Paris for a few weeks, via Geneva when we were feeling well enough, then home in time for the exam results. It all sounded fine in theory we would see how the theory turned out in practice.

The night before we were due to leave Mrs Russell held an impromptu party for us and despite the short notice just about everyone managed to make it. Mrs Russell, although she worked long hours and hardly saw any of us from one year to the next, certainly knew how to make people feel welcome and relaxed. Sue had been drafted in to prepare the food and Mrs Russell had gone out herself to buy what seemed to be a truck load of booze. By the time I arrived with my bags all packed the party was in full swing with Mrs Russell holding court in the kitchen.

"Glad you finally made it Charles I was about to come looking for you myself."

"Sorry about being late I had some last minute packing to do since we're leaving straight from here in the morning."

"Well I think you have some serious catching up to do my young friend now grab yourself a beer, Sue has the BBQ on in the back garden and I just saw Barry disappearing up the hall with young Susan but for goodness sake don't say anything to her mother." She smiled and turned her attention back to the audience.

I decided I needed something to eat and headed out to the BBQ.

"Hello Charles, all ready for the big trip then?" Sue asked busily turning sausages. "You two had better behave yourselves while your away, don't want any irate fathers chasing you halfway across Europe demanding you marry their daughters."

"No we don't what that at all."

"Speaking of behaving yourselves have you seen Susan, I told her not to go sneaking off, especially with Barry."

"Oh I think I saw her in the kitchen with Mrs Russell not long ago, Barry's gone down to the off-licence for some more supplies."

"I would have thought by the state of the fridges when I arrived there was more than enough supplies as you put it."

"Well I'm sure there is but you don't want it to get to midnight and find out there's nothing left and everything is shut now do you?"

"I suppose your right. Fancy a sausage in a roll then?"

"I thought you'd never ask." Barry was saved again.

Barry reappeared about half an hour later looking like the cat who got the cream and Susan followed along about ten minutes later. We went and sat down at the table where Sue couldn't hear us.

"You love playing dangerous games don't you?" I was sort of mad I had had to cover up for him and that he had someone who was always on to him to have sex.

"It was nothing of the sort. She just wanted to make sure I wouldn't forget her while I'm away and I certainly won't!"

"Your mother saw you two sneaking off you know."

"She's cool, she won't say anything." The night was a huge success. I ended up crashed out in the spare bedroom about three, dreaming about the weeks ahead and slipping Susan one myself as she bent over the back of the couch.

I woke up with a start and rushed into the kitchen to see what time it was, the place looked like a bomb had hit it. Shit its eight o'clock and the plane leaves in an hour and a half. I ran into Barry's bedroom come on time to get up, we should have been out of here an hour ago. Barry was not a morning person and considering the amount he had had to drink the night before it was a pretty ugly sight.

"OK OK I coming," he said and rolled over.

I called a taxi then had a quick shower. By the time I got out Barry was sitting in the kitchen looking like death warmed up drinking coffee.

"You shouldn't let me drink so much you know."

"Don't look at me I had nothing to do with that bottle of port, blame your mother."

The taxi arrived and we were on our way. The traffic was a nightmare. There was no way we were going to make that plane. We didn't. We ran into Departures at exactly nine thirty, just as the plane was due to take off. Fortunately mother had booked Business Class tickets so we checked in for the midday flight. Hair of the dog that bit us was the only solution so we settled in at the bar for the duration. It didn't take long to get back to where we had finished off last night and by the time the plane was called I was feeling somewhat worse for wear.

Playing it as straight as we could we managed to get seated on the plane and waited for take off. I hate the thought of not being able to get up and down when I wanted so I had requested a aisle seat. Barry always liked to be able to see where he was going and had the a window seat. The seat between us was still vacant when we sat down. The other thing I hated about flying was having to talk to complete strangers and especially fat strangers who insisted on spreading themselves over both of the arm rests. I watched my fellow passengers file by hoping none of them would sit down and we could have the spare seat to ourselves. I had one particularly bad scare when this huge women, who had lumbered up the isle spraying the other passengers trying to find their seats in all directions, stopped in front of me and ask whether that seat was 21E. What is it with these people not only are they ugly can't they fucking read?

"No I'm sorry mam this is 12E, 21E would be down the back somewhere in economy, I replied not looking at her.

Finally just when I thought all the passengers had boarded and the seat was indeed spare a stunning young girl came through the door. This way come and sit over here this must be your seat and if it isn't I'll have it changed. She walked past, shit. I am definitely going to have to practice my mental telepathy powers.

I hardly had time to finish the thought when from behind me she asked: "is that seat 12E?"

I jumped and turned around all at once. "I thought you had disappeared into the bowels of the aircraft."

"I'm sorry I didn't mean to frighten you, I'm afraid I wasn't concentrating on what I was doing." She had a wonderful smile.

"Don't apologise, here let me help you with those." I helped her up with the hand luggage and we sat down.

"Lolly that's a very pretty name."

"How do you know my name?"

"I just read your mind and out it came."

"I've heard it all now, you must have seen it on my luggage tag, neat trick. But I'm afraid you have an advantage over me, you know my name but I do not know yours."

"Charles, Charles Wilde and this is my friend Barry," indicating in his direction.

He had been staring out the window but when he heard his name he turned to see what was wrong. He had a finger buried knuckle deep in his right nostril. He pulled it out and stuck his hand under his leg. This was about his only annoying habit, picking his nose at the most inopportune times and more usually after he had had a few drinks. He looked embarrassed.

"This is Lolly, I said, "she'll be sitting here."

"Good, I mean nice to meet you," said Barry, not offering her his hand thank goodness. He turned back to the window.

"You'll have to excuse Barry he's had a few drinks and he just gets like that, he doesn't mean to be rude."

"Don't worry I quite understand."

"So your going to Rome too then, holiday is it?"

"No I live there with my father when I'm not at school in England but now I have finished it will become my permanent home."

"Finished? You've just done your A-Levels too?"

"Yes and you?"

"Yes, what school did you go to?"

"I doubt you would know it, its in London, Mercywood College?"

"Oh yer sure I've heard of it."

"What about you then where did you go?"

"Bailly College in Hertfordshire. Wait a minute Mercywood isn't that where all the diplomats children go?"

"I guess it must be."

"So what exactly does you father do in Rome then?"

"He's the British Ambassador."

"Come on I may look dumb but I'm not stupid. Is he really?"

"Yes really and stop staring, its not as if he is posted to Washington or anything. If you have time when your in Rome you could always drop by and I'll introduce you."

I let the subject drop and settled back for take-off, ambassador's daughter, interesting. About halfway through the flight having refused champagne each time it was offered, Barry started to lift his game and was actually adding usefully to the conversation. By the time we landed Lolly had recommended a hotel and she said on mentioning her father's name we would be looked after. Then providing the security checks went through without finding we were actually Irish terrorists or something a car would come for us tomorrow evening at eight and we would be having dinner with her and her father at the Embassy. So although things had started out less than well they had improved dramatically during the flight. We took a taxi into the city together, she dropped us off at the hotel, saying something in Italian to the doorman, leaving us watching the back of her head as the car sped away. There was definitely a spark there I thought as we checked in and were shown to our rooms, I wonder if all they say about diplomats daughters is true. We ate pizza in this little restaurant around the corner from the hotel that night, deciding to leave the exploring until the morning and get a good nights sleep instead.

I was awake early the next morning, sun streaming in through the windows and the din of the early morning traffic growing louder below. Rome and other large cities like London and Paris have an inbuilt energy which seems to drive everything and everyone in them. Being in the middle of all that energy just makes you feel so alive. I had to virtually break the door down before Barry opened it, how we were going to get on with me being a morning person and him not I was beginning to wonder. Eventually he was showered and watered and we were on our way. We hadn't actually been to Rome for about seven years so we were both rather excited to be back. As time was on our side for once I felt it would be better not to rush round and see everything in the first two days besides Rome was hugely spread out and if we did that we would be exhausted and not able to do anything. So it was off to the Coliseum first and then a leisurely lunch by the river. Rome is a strange and romantic city, not like Paris romantic but a much stronger, more male interruption of the word. The Coliseum is a perfect example of this. Here hundreds of Christians were slaughtered just for the shear pleasure of seeing them torn apart and eaten by lions and when you sit there you can almost imagine what the atmosphere would have been like. People dressed in the finest clothes, food and wine in abundance, all screaming for the lion to end the life of another helpless Christian. It would be easy to leave it at that, a place where people were sacrificed, a monument to a time long past. But that's not how the Roman's see it. It has been used for outdoor concerts and operas, the stands filled with people as they once were hundreds of years ago. Rome is alive, a living museum if you will, and as new buildings go up replacing the old the essence of the city remains strong, kept alive by the people that still proudly call themselves Romans. A long lunch and some good red wine finished the afternoon off nicely. Time to get back to the hotel and get ready for tonight.

The black stretch limousine with diplomatic plates was outside the hotel promptly at eight, the security check must have gone though without finding anything then, that was handy to know in itself. The embassy was an imposing building off one of the main streets which runs just north of the railway station. They were obviously expecting us because we were waved straight in. Walking up the beautiful stone stairs to the main entrance, the door opened and Lolly stepped out dressed in a flowing blue shaffon dress, she looked stunning and much older.

"Glad you could make it gentlemen, I almost phoned this morning to confirm then forgot completely about it." She smiled at the remembering.

"Testing our memories?" Barry said as he surveyed the grounds.

"Amongst other things. Please come in, father is expecting you. Actually we won't be dining alone tonight."

"I hope we are not putting anyone out." I hated the thought of being a nuisance.

"No of course not, we are hosting a dinner on behalf of the British Traders Association in London, frightfully boring I'm afraid, so your company will be much appreciated."

"How did you know we had arrived?"

"I had the driver ring me just before you pulled up. Couldn't have you walk in by yourselves without explaining what was going on now could we." We followed her inside.

On entering the main reception room there were small groups of men standing about talking in both English and Italian as waiters moved between the groups with hordouves. At the end of the room, standing by the fireplace, was a dashingly handsome man with a full head of grey hair, this must be her father, in fact you could see the similarities between them.

The group stopped talking and parted as she approached. "Father, sorry to disturb you, these are the two gentlemen I was telling you about, I thought you should meet before dinner, this is Mr Wilde and Mr Russell."

"But of course my dear."

"Very nice to meet you Ambassador and for allowing your daughter to invite us along tonight," Barry said.

"Well as you may have guessed my daughter pretty much decides things for herself. Now if you'll excuse me I must make sure everyone is mingling, we shall talk after everyone has left." He moved off around the room shaking hands as he went.

Dinner went smoothly, a six course feast would perhaps describe it better, I declined dessert and opted instead for coffee. Discussion around the table was subdued, no doubt hampered by the language difference, none of the English delegation spoke any Italian, as you would expect. By the end I was glad to be able to get up and retire to one of the sitting rooms.

We sat and talked until the Ambassador joined us.

"Sorry about the delay, I'm afraid these sort of receptions are all part of the job description, it just difficult to stay awake though sometimes." We all laughed.

"Can I offer you boys a glass of port with your coffee?"

"That would be very nice, thank you," I said.

He went over and pressed to button on the wall. "So what brings you to Rome then?"

"Well like your daughter we have both just finished our A-Level exams and the opportunity to do a little travelling before the results are published was too good to miss." He watched me intently as I spoke.

"Quite right as well, I've been saying the same thing to Lolly but she won't listen. Stuck here with her old father is no place for a young girl to be she should be out enjoying herself."

Just then the butler arrived with three glasses of port.

The Ambassador raised his glass: "Your good health."

"And yours." I replied. "Excellent port."

"What would you say to a travelling companion then?"

"Father! What if I don't want to go?"

"You haven't stopped talking about this young man since you got home, why would you not want to go?"

Trying to avoid any further embarrassment I said: "you don't have to make your mind up straight away we intend to be in Rome till the end of the week then we thought we would catch the train down to Naples."

"And where will you be staying down there?" the Ambassador inquired.

"I'm sure we will find a little hotel somewhere."

"I have a better idea. We have a house just a little further along the coast, why don't you take one of the cars and drive down, it's only a couple of hours and you can stay as long as you like. At least this way I know Lolly will be safe."

Lolly didn't look all that pleased that everything had been arranged without consulting her but it was too bad, a plan was in place.

"I think its time we were getting back," I said.

"I'll call for the car." The ambassador got up and pressed the button again.

When we were clear of the main gate Barry said: "I could get used to this, the driver and the car and all I mean. Oh and by the way well organised."

"Why thank you my good man."

"No I was being sarcastic, you should have asked her if she had any friends she could bring along for me."

"Sorry the thought never crossed my mind."

"No I bet it didn't."

We spent the next few days exploring Rome and on the day before we were due to leave Lolly met us by the Spanish steps and we went for coffee down the street.

"Well I hope you two have had an enjoyable week wandering around Rome."

"We have actually," I replied.

"I am sorry I could not join you but as I explained I had so many things to organise and people to see not having been back for long that it took all my time. I have directions for tomorrow and the car has been serviced ready to go. Do you think you can handle the traffic? She looked at me almost wishing me to say no.

"I guess we will find out tomorrow."

"That we will. I will send a car for you at seven tomorrow morning."

"Seven isn't that a little early?" Barry was suddenly paying attention.

"Best we are out of the city before peak hour, just be ready."

I took Barry's key from him that night so I could let myself in and wake him up. It turned out to be an unnecessary precaution because by the time I walked in he was up, dressed and ready to go. Must have been something in the water that morning. The car was out the front waiting and the driver helped us with the luggage. As we pulled up the drive of the embassy outside stood a gleaming red Alfa Romeo Spider, with her roof down, from about 1972. I had always wanted one of those and she was in beautiful condition, this was going to be a great trip.

In preparation for our drive out of Rome I had put on my black jeans and a black tee-shirt and had slicked back my hair with mousse. With black hair and dark sunglasses there was no way anyone could tell I wasn't Italian.

"You certainly look the part Charles is there anything you neglected to tell me about your parents ancestors?" Lolly was standing at the front door again as we arrived.

"I figure it's a bit like dressing for dinner, done well and it is bound to be a success, throw on jeans and a sweat shirt and something will always go wrong. Are you ready?"

"Of course."

"Then it is time we hit the road."

The traffic in Rome wasn't too bad considering how it could be and when in doubt it was just best to close your eyes and go for it, praying at the same time. We arrived in Naples about two and a half hours later, somewhat wind blown from the trip and eventually found the turning for the house on a road out in the middle of no where. Poor old Barry had suffered the most sitting in the back with virtually no leg room and even less protection. We turned in and followed the tree lined drive as it wound its way up through the gardens at the front. Turning the last corner the full splendour of the house was finally visible. A 17th-century vineyard estate house in red brick, the walls were vitally completely covered in ivy, jasmine and other creepers I did not recognise immediately.

"This is absolutely beautiful, your father gave no indication of this, I mean he didn't say anything."

"I know, I think he forgets how beautiful this place really is, he is so busy in Rome, he hardly gets down here anymore. Why don't we unpack and then I can give you a guided tour."

"Yes that would be a great idea," said Barry, "had better give us half an hour though I need to pick all the bugs out of my teeth."

We were shown to our rooms which had adjoining doors into a common bathroom. We both opened our doors at once, Barry commenting that it was rather a nice touch. In all there were eight bedrooms upstairs, remarkably none being all that different in size from the others. Downstairs there was a formal sitting room off one side of the entrance hall which lead directly into the formal dinning room and judging by the number of chairs it could seat almost twenty people, Italians and large families I guess. Another two informal sitting rooms came off the other side of the hall, the furthest leading though to the breakfast room. Large French doors opened up onto a huge paved area, which like the house was covered in flowering vines. Pots with flowers spilling out almost stood at attention surrounding a wooden outdoor setting the size of which I had never encountered before in my life.

Lolly began to explain. "The people who used to live here and actually built the house almost three hundred years ago worked the vineyards themselves and so having a large family to be able to do all of this work was part of the family tradition, hence the size of the dining room and this table. We believe that the timber for the table, like the house itself, was all grown and sawn here. The bricks were all hand made and fired in an oven, the remains of which can be seen behind the wall of the vegetable garden. It is incredible to think that those people made this house with their bare hands so long ago and yet it is still standing for us to enjoy."

"What happened to them?" I asked.

"The last generation could not decide what to do with the property once the father died, the majority of the sons wanted to do other things and the rest did not have the money to buy the others out so they finally agreed to sell it about the time my parents arrived from England and it has been in the family ever since."

Barry went off to explore the wine processing sheds and cellars. Lolly and I went for a walk in the garden.

"You said parents before what happened to your mother?"

"She died only a couple of years ago."

"I'm sorry I didn't mean to pry."

"No I am fine about it now, not so when it first happened. She got cancer of the ovaries and in the end there was really nothing they could do for her. At first they weren't sure what it was, she had weeks of tests before they found the growth. She was immediately scheduled to have it removed and when they found it to be malignant they carried out a full hysterectomy. The doctors were confident, they said they thought they had removed all the infected tissue and that the chemotherapy would deal with what little they may of missed. I think the hardest thing for me was watching all her beautiful hair fall out, I know she cried herself to sleep over that particularly. It's funny she used to wear this Dodgers baseball cap everywhere she went, of course it was only funny to me because I knew how much she hated the game. It was her attempt at irony. She died six months later. The night she died though it was almost as if she was her old self again, laughing, joking, she even looked better. They say it just happens like that sometimes."

"I know."

"What do you mean you know have you ever had to watch while someone you love and can never replace dies?" She looked at me with thunder clouds looming in her face.

"Yes, no, I don't know. Oh I wish I had never said anything now."

"No go on you started it now finish it."

"You have to promise me not to tell Barry."

"I promise." She still looked annoyed.

"About two months ago I had to go into hospital to have my wisdom teeth out. Anyway on the first night I went out for a wander just to get out of the room really and as I was heading back a young girl called me into her room. Anyway to cut a long story short, we talked for a while, the lights went out, she grabbed my arm as I was about to leave and we kissed. When I went back a couple of days later after my operation she was gone. I did not think all that much about it until as we were leaving one of the nurses said she had died two nights ago. It would seem she had been suffering from leukaemia for years and that night, the night I had kissed her, her body just gave up. I haven't told anyone about this, not even my parents, in fact I have been trying to forget it but it just won't go away."

"Sounds as if you were a gift from heaven, everything she had ever dreamed about came true in the short time you were with her. She was complete, she was able to go in peace." The look on her face had softened.

"You really think so?"

"Yes I do, I am glad you told me though, it seems we have quite a bit in common. Now time for happier thoughts, how about I make us some lunch, we can sit outside, what do you say?"

"Sounds perfect, I wonder if Barry has found any wine yet."

"Well if he has failed to find wine here I think he is going to need glasses, desperately." We laughed a little and headed back to the house.

Sure enough Barry had managed to find some wine, in fact some very good wine. He insisted that I had to come with him after lunch and see the cellars, he said there was more wine stored down there than you could drink in a lifetime. Lolly explained that they still make wine here each year, her father had bought in a local manager who looked after the whole place. They then sold only enough to clear the running expenses and despite using some at the Embassy they still managed to have a surplus each year and that's what Barry had seen. We ate sitting at one end of the huge wooden table, making rolls with the baked ham and cheese we had bought in a little village on the way. For the rest of the afternoon it was really too hot to do anything but lie around and read waiting for the evening to come and dinner. Over the next four weeks we repeated this ritual, walking in the early morning, lunch, reading or swimming in the afternoon and then dinner outside at the table.

Nothing happened between Lolly and I and nothing looked like it was going to happen. It's strange how when the thing you most want is suddenly there in front of you, your are unable or unwilling to do anything about it. I think it has something to do with dreams. What if everything you had ever dreamed about suddenly came true? What would you do then? So it was with Lolly.

This routine was only interrupted by some sightseeing in the local area of which Pompeii was the most haunting and swimming into the Grotta Azzura at sunset on Capri was the most spectacular. The Grotta Azzura as the name suggests was a cave which turned the most intense blue colour I have ever seen in my life at sunset and that is where we kissed for the first time, two days before we were due to leave.

"I was sort of hoping that was not going to happen but now it has I am glad. I used to come swimming here with my mother when I was a little girl, it is a very special place to me."

"Well you are a very special person, I'm not looking forward to having to leave at the end of the week. Do you think you father would let you come with us to Munich?"

"I do not think he will have a problem with that providing we travel first class, he gets nervous about what might happen to me otherwise."

"Fine then back to Rome Friday and then off to Munich."

We swam out of the cave together in the fading light and watched the sun complete its decent before swimming back.

Friday morning we said goodbye to the house and were in Rome inside two hours. Lolly cleared the trip with her father without too much argument and he gave her money enough to upgrade our tickets to First Class. The next day we bid farewell to the Ambassador and bordered the train for Milan. There we would change for Zurich where we would catch the over night train to Munich. I was really looking forward to the beer feast having never been before and yet heard so many stories of what happens there. Besides I would begin to look like a grape if I drank any more wine. We managed to pick up the connecting train to Zurich despite the unpredictability of the Italian rail network and sat spell bound as we picked our way through the Italian Alps. The men that built these lines risked everything for a few shillings just so the trains could get through. The designers had a great vision and will to make things happen, I doubt if someone suggested today to build a railway through such an inhospitable place that it would ever happen. We arrived in Zurich only slightly late and soon we were on our way to Munich on the highly efficient Swiss rail system. We had dinner in the dining car and then retired early. Nothing really to do on a train once the sun goes down.

We arrived in Munich early the next morning having had a wonderful breakfast in the dining car beforehand and set off in search of a modest priced hotel. Lolly seemed to know her way around and had even thought to bring a map of the city with her, so we followed along behind as she led the way.

We stopped outside this beautiful old hotel which from the outside looked very expensive. "This looks fine doesn't it?" And without waiting for a reply she took off up the stairs and disappeared inside. I turned to look at Barry who was standing there with a very disturbed look on his face.

"I don't think we can afford this you know," he said.

"I was thinking the same thing, I'll go and find her and explain."

When I went inside Lolly was standing by the reception desk, hands on her hips, holding three room keys, staring at me as I walked through the door.

"Are you two quite ready?"

"I don't know if this is the best place to stay do you, it looks rather expensive."

A smile came to her face. "Oh bless him. Perhaps I should of told you, father booked this hotel for us yesterday and has already arranged to have the bill forwarded to him so stop worrying. You do realise that at this time of year unless he had there was no way we would have found anywhere to stay, these hotels are usually booked months in advance. And there is no need to thank him either. It was just his way of making sure we didn't have to sleep in the same bed in the youth hostel."

"That wouldn't have been so bad would it?"

"In your dreams perhaps."

By this time Barry had begun to wonder what had happened to us and came wandering into reception. Lolly took great pleasure in explaining the situation and watching the deeply worried look disappear from his face.

The rooms were lovely, each having their own wooden four poster beds with canopies. We hurriedly unpacked and took a taxi outside the hotel for the beer feast.

From the third Saturday in September till the end of October, Munich is packed with tourists, all with one thing on their mind, drinking as much beer as possible. In fact more beer is drunk in the five weeks of the *Oktoberfest* than is consumed in Britain in an entire year. This sounded like our kind of city. We paid our entrance fee and walked through the gates. All around the smell of cooking food pervaded your senses and music could be heard coming from the huge drinking tents which stretched out across the site. I suggested that we head for the Australian tent as I had heard it was the loudest and the best places to drink. Following the guide we eventually found the tent. Like all the others it was filled with long wooden benches and seats and everyone was sitting down singing along to the Umppapa Band playing on the stage. We found a seat on the end of one of the tables and waited to be served, I was starting to get a real thirst on. We were finally served, the waitress bringing three huge steins of beer back with her. They soon disappeared. We sat there the whole day drinking, only stopping to send someone out for hot-dogs or roast chicken. As the day wore on the entire tent population got more and more drunk until it became impossible for the staff to stop people standing on the tables, dancing and singing. I was surprised at how well Lolly kept up the pace, she had obviously had some serious drinking practice. Towards the end there were lines of girls on the stage in front of the band pulling up their beer soaked tee shirts as the crowd cheered them on, it was absolutely outrageous. Barry kept disappearing every so often, more often than not returning with a huge smile on his face. The last time I remember him going he returned with a stunning looking Australian girl on his arm, I decided I was too drunk to bother finding out who she was. By the end of the night we could hardly stand and Lolly insisted she had had enough to drink and it was time to go home. Barry and Kelly, I found her name out the next day, decided they would stay for a little while longer so we left them to it

We stumbled into the hotel foyer to be greeted by a disgusted look from the night porter and got our keys.

"Why don't you come back to my room and I'll order coffee, I think we could both use some don't you?"

"I think your right but I won't stay long I really need some sleep."

We eventually found my room and unlocked the door. The bed looked so inviting after the days events and we both must have been thinking the same thing because without saying a word we crossed the room and flopped down on to it, falling immediately to sleep.

Sometime during the night I sat up in bed, I had been dreaming I was dead and had just watched my own funeral, the room was completely black. I could hear all these things breathing all around me but none of the sounds were mine. I really was dead. I sat there, not daring to move and broke out in a cold sweat. What the fuck am I supposed to do now? All of a sudden there was a movement on the floor beside the bed, I nearly pissed myself.

"You all right mate?" My eyes had adjusted to the darkness slightly and I was just able to make out a shape sitting up on the floor. I really was dead and there were other dead people in here with me. The figure laid down again and all I could hear was the breathing. I decided to make a break for the bathroom, if it was still there. In one swift movement I jumped out of the end of the bed, shot across the room to where the bathroom should have been and ran straight into the closed door. I grabbed for the handle, opened the door, slammed it behind me and turned on the light. I looked in the mirror, it was not a pretty sight but I was alive. I went to the toilet, took of my clothes and stepped into the shower, I was in dire need. I stood under the hot water and let the warmth flow over me, I began to feel much better. Just as I was about to step out in walked Kelly stark naked. What the hell was she doing here? I don't think she was really awake because she paid me no attention at all. She walking up to the bidet right beside the shower and instead of sitting down simple relieved herself standing there while I watched, then she turned and walked out again. Shit that was horny.

Before I came out of the bathroom again I opened the door so I could see into the room and reassure myself that I wasn't dead and find out what the hell was going on. The figure on the floor had been Barry and the door between our two rooms was wide open. They must have been so drunk by the time they got back that they had opened it thinking the bedroom was in there and had fallen asleep on the floor when they discovered someone was already in the bed. Kelly wasn't on the floor anymore though she was lying on the bed next to Lolly, I decided I had seen enough, switched the light out and went back to bed. I lay down next to Kelly trying not to disturb her.

"Enjoy the show then, all the boys at home like that one." She had been awake.

Without saying anything more she took hold of my dick and started to play with me. After a while she moved down the bed and began giving me a blow job, I could just make out the shape of her head as it went up and down. She was very good but I was afraid she would wake Lolly, I didn't think I would ever see her again if she woke up now. Despite these worry I soon felt my balls tighten as I came in her mouth. She came back and laid beside me. "I think you needed that."

Before I could reply she leaned over me and turned on the light beside the bed.

"Don't do that you'll wake the others up."

"No need to worry about that they're completely out of it. I think it's time for some fun don't you?" Her face hovered only inches from mine as she looked into my eyes.

"I thought that's what we just had."

"No I mean some real fun."

She got off the bed and walked round the other side, kneeling down beside Lolly. She looked over at me and then started undressing Lolly. Shit. She must have had some practice at this because in a few minutes Lolly was lying there, still asleep without a thing on. She came back and knelt beside me and whispered in my ear.

"I think your girlfriends beautiful don't you? I wonder how far we can get before she wakes up? I want you to get up, go round the other side and just watch."

By the time I walked round the bed Kelly was already beginning to move her legs apart. She stirred. Lolly stopped and we both stayed perfectly still. She didn't wake. Kelly continued. She eventually had Lolly legs wide apart and then came round and stood beside me.

"Don't you think she has a lovely pussy? Look its just lying there waiting for us to play with it." My erection had returned with a vengeance and she grabbed hold of it and pulled me down until we were both kneeling beside Lolly. She glanced at me quickly then bent forward and ran the tip of her tongue up the length of Lolly's leg, just stopping short of her crotch. She looked at me again. She then took a finger and circled the small patch of pubic hair which adorned the top of her crack. She motioned for me to do the same. My hand shook as I touched her skin. I pulled my hand away and Kelly leaned over and kissed me. We knelt there for a few moments, my head was reeling. Then she reached over and ever so slowly parted Lolly's lips with one hand. Then she bought the other hand up and began to tease her clit.

Lolly moved again slightly but still didn't wake. "There she may be asleep but she is enjoying that, I wonder what she tastes like?"

She dipped her fingers into her slit and then bought one hand up to her mouth. "Nectar of the God's, here," and she offered another to me. She put her hand back between Lolly's legs, this time rubbing her a bit harder, she slipped two fingers inside and just then Lolly turned over towards us. I jumped. Kelly's hand was still between her legs.

We stayed very still as Kelly mastibated her, little groans coming from deep inside Lolly's chest.

I slipped my hand between Kelly's legs and she sat on me fingers. "I think that's about all we are going to see tonight," she said, removing her hand slowly.

We moved away from the bed and pushing her down on the floor I mounted her. "Your a very bad girl."

"I know and you love it." She was right. I fucked her hard with long deliberate strokes. Just as I was about to come she bought her hands round, grabbed my cheeks, spread them apart and shoved a finger up my arse. I had the most powerful orgasm of all time. She was certainly full of surprises.

After we had finished, she kissed me, thanked me for an unforgettable evening, dressed and left, I fell asleep where I lay. I woke just before the other two and managed to find my clothes in the bathroom and dress before they started to stir. I didn't have the heart to tell Barry what had happened when he asked where Kelly was and I was certainly not going to tell Lolly, not yet anyway. We all felt pretty rough that morning and decided to skip any beer drinking until that evening. Actually we never did get as drunk again as that first night, waking up and thinking you are dead is not something I didn't want to repeat.

I had trouble looking at Lolly in quite the same way after that night. I wondered what her reaction would be if she knew what had happened with Kelly. She could have two distinctly different reactions. Either she would be extremely turned on by the story or completely disgusted and never talk to me again, I decided not to take the risk.

We left for Paris at the end of the week, Munich had been a blast but I needed to get out of there and get my head straight. Paris really is the city of romance. It is a delicate and beautiful city, full of expectation and life. I couldn't help but wonder if this is where I would finally find out if Lolly was to be the one. Her father's hand hadn't quite reached this far and we booked into a modest hotel on the south bank. That first night we left Barry in the hotel complaining of a bad stomach and we went out for dinner alone. It was really the first time we had been by ourselves, I wondered if we would be able to find things to talk about for the whole evening. As it turned out we did and had a lovely meal. We walked back to the hotel along the Seinewhich seemed to sparkle under the streets lights.

"You know it could never work between us". Lolly had stopped and was looking out across the river at a cruise boat going by. "Do you ever wonder when you look at a boat like that where all these people are from and where they're going to?"

"Wait a minute, don't change the subject, what do you mean?"

"Well your going off to university next year and my life is in Rome, I can not see it working."

"How do you come to that conclusion, besides nothing has happened between us, I mean we only kissed once, you haven't even given it a chance."

"I know nothing happened between us because I decided I did not want to take the risk of becoming too involved in something that I may regret later."

"Wait a minute don't I get a say in all this after all it does take two to make a regret, or is that to tango, I can't remember."

"I'm sorry, I'll be flying back to Rome tomorrow and the best thing you can do is forget we ever met."

"Tomorrow, but we were supposed to be here for a week."

"I know but I spoke to my father this afternoon and he has arranged a ticket for me tomorrow. I want you to know that I will always remember this holiday, it has been just perfect, but I really must get back. Please don't make it more difficult than it already is."

"Difficult?" I was fuming, how could she simply dismiss me just like that, I hadn't even been given a proper chance. We walked back to the hotel in silence.

The next morning she had her bags packed and was waiting at reception when we came down. The taxi arrived.

"I will always remember you Charles Wilde, thank you for being a wonderful friend." Those were the last words I ever heard her speak, she climbed into the taxi and sped off into the morning traffic.

I stood there on the pavement for a long time looking out in the direction in which she had left, half expecting the taxi to come back the other way and for her to jump out and run into my arms. It never happened.

After much drinking and consoling each other Barry and I decided we had had enough travelling and caught a plane home the next day ourselves.

Samantha Epilogue

It is not as you said it would be,
but I am still waiting.
Richard Overcome

Thoughout the flight home I went over and over in my mind the weeks that had just past. That first meeting on the plane, dinner at the Embassy, Naples, Munich and finally Paris. What had I done wrong? Should I have been more forceful, should I have been more dismissive. Perhaps she had interpreted my attention simply as friendship, she couldn't have been further from the truth. Not since Susan had I felt so comfortable with another person, but perhaps that was the trouble, comfort leads to complacency and perhaps that's what she feared or was it simply the commitment?

We landed at Heathrow and mother was there to pick us up.

"Charles you looked wonderful," she said as she kissed me walking out of arrivals. "I can't help but think you look older, more grown up but that must be just my imagination, you've only been gone six weeks. Did you enjoy yourselves?"

"We had a wonderful time, one we are unlikely to forget." Well there was no point burdening her with all my problems.

"I have a surprise waiting for you at home."

"Oh yer what is it, a car?"

"You'll just have to wait and see."

As we pulled into the driveway I expected to see a shiny new four wheel drive sitting there waiting for me, it was no where in sight.

"Is it in the garage then," I asked.

"Come on in side and we'll see."

But instead of four wheel drive sitting in the garage, Sam was sitting in the kitchen.

"I've missed you," she said getting up for the table.

She walked over to me, put her arms around my neck, I drew her close and we kissed. Maybe something has to be taken away from you before you realise what you had to begin with.

Copyright

ISBN 978-1-4461-3605-8